# WRITIN' ON EMPTY

Darren,
we're all in
this together—
Enjoy the
ride!
Julie
8/08

Cover: Shelby Designs & Illustrates

Authors' photo: Bruce Nye (with 1971 Mercury Cougar convertible courtesy of Joel Cehn)

Layout: Alvaro Villanueva

No Flak Publishing

Printed in the United States of America

ISBN: 978-0-6152-0885-5

# Writin' On Empty:

## Parents Reveal the Upside, Downside, and Everything in Between When Children Leave the Nest

EDITED BY

*Joan Cehn, Risa Nye, and Julie Renalds*

**No Flak Publishing**

*"All the art of living lies in a fine mingling of letting go and holding on."*

—*Henry Ellis*

*To Amy, Michelle, Caitlin, Myles, and James: The door is always open.*

# Contents

Writin' on Empty delivers the "upside, downside, and everything in between," its title promises. This collection of essays about the universal experience of children leaving home is guaranteed to strike a chord—to make you smile and laugh out loud—and yes, even shed some tears. It will confirm what you've been thinking as well as challenge you to think a bit differently. A diverse group of writers—both those who write for a living and those who simply love to write—reflect on the "emptying nest"—each in a distinctive voice. This is not a "how to" book, it's a volume that captures "how it is." You'll want to mark it up with exclamation points and your own thoughts—and return to your favorite entries again and again.

—Karen Levin Coburn co-author,
*Letting Go: A Parents' Guide to Understanding the College Years*

# INTRODUCTION

IT'S LIKE THE TREE FALLING in the forest when no one is around: When your kids leave home, are you still a parent? If no one yells "Hey, Mom!" (or Dad) on a daily basis, does your primary identity undergo a major change? It's a strange business, raising kids. If you do your job reasonably well, the idea is that they will leave you and go out on their own. For eighteen years or so, ever since your baby's first cry, you are tuned in to her every move and mood: each tear, each skinned knee ... right up to the first time behind the wheel, the first slammed door, and the first date. Then, one day, the kids leave: some for college, some to don a uniform and join the service, some to follow a dream, and some to find space to grow. And now you are standing in the doorway of a vacant bedroom, feeling the silence and emptiness as it echoes through your home. You should be able to sleep easy, not waiting for that car to pull up or that door to slam again. But maybe you can't. Maybe you discover that missing your child has turned into an ache that can't be touched. Or, perhaps your child has made a successful transition and you are already leafing through design books or travel brochures and planning the rest of your life. Maybe it was easier than you thought it was going to be. I handled that pretty well, you think ... and then you get a phone call that begins with a catch in the throat: "Mommy..."

Back in the day, parents would talk over the fence about these things. Maybe there would be a club or a meeting where the subject would come up. In our mobile society, we can no longer count on our friends and neighbors staying put from kindergarten to graduation. But we still learn best from the stories we tell each other. We may scoff at so-called experts, but a neighbor's cousin's best friend's experience may resonate with us in a way that gives us comfort and assurance that we, too, will be able to move ahead with our lives after the kids have gone. And while we can't get the story from everyone, in Writin' on Empty we have tried to create a community for other parents who are bemoaning their silent houses and empty bedrooms. On the other hand, those who choose to start redecorating as soon as the nest empties out will discover that they are not alone either.

According to the US Census, there are over sixteen million young people enrolled in colleges and universities today. That's a lot of good-byes and "see you at Thanksgivings." What was it like for those families when the oldest, the youngest, or the one and only packed up and left? Each year, for the last several years, over three million kids graduated from high school. Again, plenty of tissues and care packages as those three million strong took off for college, work, travel, or uncertainty. How do parents manage these transitions? Where do they turn for help—or reassurance?

As three mothers of college-age kids, we found that there was a real need for stories like ours to circulate. We could see the concern in the faces of parents on the verge, and we wanted to help. Julie Renalds used her professional skills to gather parents together to talk about what Julie called "Post-Partum Part Deux." Through this discussion group, Julie met Joan Cehn, who had just sent her only child off to college and was going through a tough separation. Joan and Julie believed that the exchange of stories was soothing and healing, and wondered if they could reach even more people through more stories. Joan's long-time friend Risa Nye is a Bay Area writer and had successfully ushered her three children off to college. Risa stood by Joan during her separation process and was delighted with the prospect of helping Julie and Joan nurture their idea into book form.

We cast a wide net for stories, using local contacts to get started. We ultimately got essays from people we know, people we don't know, and published authors we admire. We have essays from Bay Area writers Ronnie Caplane, C.W. Nevius, Elizabeth Fishel, and Linda Lee Peterson. Greatly revered columnist Al Martinez of the *Los Angeles Times*, winner of many prestigious journalism awards, contributed essays. Linda Weltner, for many years an award-winning columnist at the *Boston Globe,* is heard here, as is John Leland of the *New York Times*. Some of our other writers are previously unpublished, while some have been writing for years. Although we didn't ask any personal questions, we feel pretty sure that Martha Loeffler, in her 80s, is our most senior contributor. We are parents and grandparents, mothers and fathers, single, married, and divorced.

Above all, we are storytellers and we have a lot to share with a parent who even now may be taking down the scrapbook or photo album and shedding a few tears over that nearly grown girl or boy who just yesterday took a first independent step. We have seen time after time that new doors open when the front door closes—after our sons and daughters travel toward their next adventure.

Finally, it is our hope that these stories will encourage you to share your own story with others. We believe that as parents, this rite of passage—letting go—is one that should not be shouldered alone. █

PART ONE

# THE UPSIDE OF EMPTY

# Naked Parents in the Pool

· *Linda Lee Peterson* ·

FIVE WEEKS, SIX DAYS, 23 HOURS AND 15 MINUTES after we delivered our son, Ben (aka Sacred Precious), to USC to begin his freshman year, I turned to a life of violence.

My husband and I had agreed, as we said good-bye to SP in late August, to fly him home for the long Veterans' Day weekend. In case he was homesick. Or needed more socks. Or we were decompensating. Or whatever. But on that fateful day, when I moved from pacifism to action, I stood in the hallway sorting through the mail, and my husband said, "You know, honey, it seems silly to fly Ben home for the weekend in November, when he'll be coming just a few weeks later for Thanksgiving."

I took one deep breath, scooped all the mail off the hall table, and hurled it at him. Then, I burst into tears. Fortunately, that day's mail did not include a mega-catalog from Sears or Neiman-Marcus, so no one had to call the cops to report domestic violence.

Between sobs, I wondered how the man who had been reduced to tears himself when listening to sappy commercials in his car could be so callous. Both of us had sat bolt upright at breakfast or dinner, more than a few times since SP left and said, "Did you hear Ben? I thought I heard his voice?" And then we'd both sigh, and say, "Oh, right. He's gone."

You get the picture. Two doting parents and one kid who had reinvented what it meant to be an only child. Only grandchild for most of his life. Only nephew of a completely indulgent aunt. This was a child who never had to buy a car, because said aunt would simply pass along her used Mustang convertibles. When he decided he liked chocolate chip cookies, but not nuts therein, I'd carefully bite the nuts out and deliver the nut-free pieces to him. His father would take a day off every summer as soon as the weather got hot and take Ben and his grade school buddies to play hooky at some cheesy waterslide park. My parents stood in line for hours to buy a first-edition ET for Ben. In leather, not vinyl, I might add. It would be an understatement to say the world revolved around SP—a nickname given to him when my business partner, clearly sick of All-Ben, all-the-time talk radio, one day asked, "How are things over at the Sepulcher of the Sacred Precious where that kid goes to school?"

So, when the little prince left, Mom and Dad initially exhibited classic signs of meltdown. Unexplained tears. Painful peeks into his astonishingly tidy bedroom. Way too much affection lavished on the dog.

But then, late one night, things began to change. It was an unseasonably warm fall that year, and we had not yet installed air-conditioning in our house. So, on particularly hot and sticky nights, we had evolved the custom of taking a very late night swim in our backyard pool. And, since there was no one to see us but the dog, we didn't bother climbing into suits. It seemed an eminently practical—and okay, a little bit fun—way to cool down before bed.

As we splashed peacefully in the pool one night, I heard the phone ring, grabbed a towel, and dashed into the house to get it. It was Ben, checking in. "Why are you out of breath, Mom?"

"Dad and I were in the pool," I reported. "I ran for the phone, thinking it was you." Silence. I added helpfully, "It's really hot here."

Ben was still silent.

"Is something wrong, honey?"

"You and Dad are nude, aren't you? In the pool, I mean."

"As a matter of fact..." I began.

"Never mind," he said. "Too much information. Naked parents in the pool, I just don't need to have a picture of that in my head."

And in that moment, I realized that the empty-nest deal had some upsides. And the gloom began to lift.

I went back to the pool after the call. Ken still lazed in the water, looking up at the stars. An owl hooted. It was so peaceful, so private.

I eased back in the pool. "It was Ben."

"What's up?" he asked.

"Nothing special," I replied. "But he's a little grossed out imagining us naked in the pool."

The moonlight illuminated Ken's face, and I watched a grin start. "He is, is he? Isn't that just too bad."

That was just the beginning of figuring out the cool deals an empty nest had to offer.

The whole clothes-optional angle was brand-new to me. No longer did I need to throw on a robe before I could pad down the hall from the bedroom to the laundry room to find clean underwear. There were other, unexpected pleasures as well. It was easier to fight! I had grown up with a mother who would gently interrupt every time a discussion got even mildly heated around the dinner table, and say, in her cultured, Southern voice, "Now, let's not have any unpleasantness."

That led me to conclude that it would be psychologically devastating for SP to ever, ever, ever hear his Mother and Dad exchange a harsh word. So, if we were disagreeing, we'd snipe, and then escalate to fierce whispers—until I'd say, "We'll discuss this later!" All of which resulted in frustration, very unsatisfying fights, and nary a slammed door. Oh, the liberty of disagreeing aloud, in whatever room we wished, whenever we wished. In fact, it seemed to me we began having shorter, more satisfying, easier-to-resolve differences of opinion. Out loud.

Plus, there was enormous Fridge Freedom. No set dinner hour, no planning ahead, lots of impulse decisions as one of us called from the car on the way home. "Go out? Cobble something together from the fridge? Scrambled eggs? Fruit and cheese?" Best of all, our favorite decadent dinner—artichokes, cracked crab, sourdough, and a really good bottle of chardonnay—was an option limited only by crab season, and not by a teenager who ate shrimp and shark, and nothing else from the sea.

And did I mention the sheer joy of breaking our own rules? I'd always preached the evils of eating in front of the television and had allowed it only during Monday Night Football, the Academy Awards, or for a movie night. Now, with little Miss Culture Dominatrix (that would be me) off-duty, and the joys of TiVo, we could sit upstairs, crack our crab, sip our chardonnay, and gorge on *The Sopranos* or *Desperate Housewives* or some over-the-top, lachrymose Irish Tenors special. It began to feel as if we were on permanent vacation.

We still are. I breathed in that realization just a few weeks ago when we visited our son, daughter-in-law, and our first, oh-so-beautiful grandchild. The baby (whom my daughter-in-law immediately dubbed SP II, demonstrating her forbearance and sense of humor) was only ten days old, and his accoutrement—from a zillion or two stuffed animals to diapers to baby seat to books, books, and more books—had more or less taken over the entire household. My son looked around, a little apologetically. "I'm sure we'll figure out how to get the house back to normal soon."

"I'm sure you will, honey," I said, thinking to myself, in just about eighteen years. EMINSTR

# THE SON REPLACEMENT DOG

· *Pam Muramatsu* ·

I WASN'T PARTICULARLY SURPRISED that I cried when we left my son, Dan, off at college. I had been feeling tearily nostalgic since I put together a scrapbook for his high school graduation. Scrapbooking is a popular form of torture these days. As I went through boxes of babyhood mementos, preschool works of art, countless report cards and notes from teachers, school pictures, family pictures, and all sorts of accomplishments, I saw the eighteen years that had passed before my eyes. Suddenly, I realized this time had gone much faster than I had ever bargained for, and I was getting the distinct feeling that perhaps my time had been, somehow, cut short. I certainly wasn't done yet. Wait! I'm not done yet! But here I was and it was too late. It was the end of an era in my life—it was my favorite era—my first-born was going ever onward and my debut and career as a young mother was over. No matter how much I wanted to keep the gig going, I was done ... or at the very least I was put on notice that my job was being phased out. There was nothing left for me to do but cry.

In the weeks that followed in my now emptier household, I soon realized that I was the only one having a hard time with the change in the parenting role. Dan settled into college life with no qualms and not even a hint of homesickness. My husband seemed accepting of what I am sure he considered the natural progression of things. I definitely wanted my baby back, but short of that I concluded that I had one more here in the nest that I could still nurture. My youngest son, barely taking notice that his older brother was absent, shrugged off my attempts to double up my mothering on him. Once sharing the spotlight, I thought Jeff might delight in suddenly being a solo show. He now had my complete and undivided attention, and I was anxious to know all about his day ... what would he like best for dinner? How was his lunch today? What would he like to do on the weekend? What were his friends up to? Jeff soon learned to deftly ignore my attentions and keep me at a safe distance. He became an aloof teenager. Despite my best efforts, I now had two babies to miss.

My solution for recapturing a piece motherhood lost came to me in the form of a little five-pound Manchester Terrier Toy puppy. My husband seemed relieved when we left the breeder, dog in my arms. I promptly named him Butch after my son's college mascot. I joked with people that this was my "son replacement dog," and after years of being a stay at home mom, I now boasted that I had a "full-time dog." My family collectively ignored me as I kept constant company with my new baby, taking him with me everywhere I could, experimenting with what clothing he would let me dress him in, sewing blankets for him and keeping him wrapped tight when it was cold, and buying him every little toy and new treat the pet store had to offer. He had all the best canine accessories. Happily, I had our picture taken on Santa's lap and bought the Christmas picture cards to send out. He followed me around all day just for the moment I would sit down and he could keep my lap warm; he slept soundly at night right between my husband and me. He was always there for me and up for a walk or a rousing game of fetch or "chase me." And even though I was never one for "baby talk" with my natural children, with my Butchy-bu I just exploded with it.

Of course, a dog is not a baby and I learned the hard way that a babied dog makes a rather miserable specimen in terms of obedience training. After many turns at obedience classes, I learned that I will never be a good dog trainer and Butch will probably never be a well-trained dog. But more importantly, he certainly does for me what I need him to. He accepts my love and coddling shamelessly. He guards, protects, and comforts me whenever I need him to. He frets for me when we are separated from each other and when we are reunited he literally jumps up and down with pure joy—even if I have only just returned from the mailbox! He keeps me going and keeps me company and he doesn't mind being my baby. He has saved my sons from the embarrassment of me and he has saved me from my tears. Best of all, he's not going to college. EMTNSTR

# College Bound Times Two

· *Martha Loeffler* ·

WE HAD DECIDED if "it" were a boy he would be named David Michael. When "it" surprised us by turning out to be identical twin boys, my husband and I scrambled to come up with middle names and soon announced that we were the proud parents of David Alan and Michael Gene Loeffler, born just three minutes apart on July 3, 1950.

From infancy they did everything together. They passed childhood colds and assorted ailments back and forth as though sharing precious jewels. When one got hurt the other also cried, and they developed a language we could not interpret. They were Bar Mitzvah (that Jewish rite of passage) together, became Eagle Scouts together, and both were members of their high school honor society as well as the cross-country and wrestling teams. No matter how differently they were dressed they still looked like the proverbial two peas in a pod. Their days of twin-identity were capped by a picture in our local paper that showed them escorting identical twin girls to their high school Senior Prom in 1968. Although we had always tried to treat them as unique individuals, we were not always successful.

They both chose to go to the University of California at Davis, but when it was time to make housing applications they informed us of their momentous decision: they elected to be in the same dormitory but in different rooms and have different roommates! Even though we had arranged to have them in separate classrooms from kindergarten on, now, for the first time in their lives, they were not going to be living together, they were not going to share the same daily experiences, and might not even see each other for days on end. I wondered how they would adjust.

It was while thinking about their impending separation that it hit me: after being busily involved in all the planning and shopping and talk of campus life, the time had come when my husband and I were going to have an empty nest! The focus of our lives was about to be changed all at once and I suddenly wondered how *we* would adjust.

The 100-mile drive from our home in Modesto to the university campus was filled with backseat chatter about class assignments, meeting new roommates, and signing up for athletic activities. My husband and I were mostly silent as we listened to the excitement in the two young voices that filled the car. And then we arrived at the dorm. Suitcases and typewriters, bicycles and boxes of bedding, and knick-knacks were all quickly unloaded. We met the new roommates and then, too soon, we were saying good-bye. As we started home, I glanced back and saw our sons standing together and waving forlornly (I thought), but when we made one more turn out of the parking lot they were already almost out of sight, exuberantly dashing back into the dorm and the beginning of a new chapter in their lives.

The ride home that day was a very quiet one. Occasionally I glanced at my husband as he drove, and when I saw his glistening eyes, I tried to divert him with small talk, but my voice wasn't steady enough to do that. When we finally walked into the house, he stopped, put his arms around me, and said in a stentorian voice, "THIS HOUSE SURE IS QUIET!" And so began the new chapter in *our* lives.

At the time, my husband, a scientist and agricultural chemist, was the department head of a research team for a major corporation. He loved his work and looked forward to each day in the laboratory. His weekends were filled with hobbies of woodwork and gardening and completing the tasks on my "Honey Do" list of things that needed fixing around the house. Although he missed the boys, he quickly accepted our new lifestyle.

I was the typical mother/housewife of the 1950s and 1960s. Even though I was a college graduate with an advanced degree in social work and had worked until our marriage, the thought of employment outside our home did not occur to me. I was very happy with my role as a wife and mother raising two future "Baby Boomers," although now part of that job description was no longer relevant. My hobbies, including playing the piano, reading, a daily swim, and actively volunteering in a variety of organizations, were the usual kind of thing that occupied the spare time of many women in those years. In addition, David and Michael came home at appropriate times and telephoned often enough to keep us informed and worry-free. For a long time, I was quite content and fulfilled—even in my empty nest.

However, as the years rolled by, I began to realize that I had "been there, done that" too many times over and I became restless. Then one morning, I read a small item in our paper detailing the need for "Readers" who would assist English teachers in local high schools by reading and correcting student essays written for homework assignments. Prospective Readers would have to pass a written test and would be paid $1.00/hour. The reading part sounded interesting, could be done at home, and apparently was not overly time-consuming, so I applied, passed the test, and was introduced to the lady I would assist, Martha Knight. Mrs. Knight didn't know it but she was about to have an enormous influence on my life.

I liked reading and correcting the students' papers and particularly enjoyed the contact and conversations with "my" teacher. Occasionally, Mrs. Knight, a talented writer herself, would show me a story she had written and I felt privileged to discuss it with her.

One day I said, "I wish I could write. I've always thought I would like to."

She responded, "Why don't you?"

"I've never taken a writing course and I don't even know how to start."

"Start with one word at a time and write what you know about." It sounded logical and not too difficult.

It was the holiday season, and as I was ready to mail cards and packages I noted the many changes in my address book. That was something I knew about, having moved around the country many times while my husband was "going up the corporation ladder." I started writing, one word at a time, as instructed. I wrote about retirement homes and new widows and recently acquired "significant others," and the myriad transitions resulting in address changes that had taken place over the years. It took a while, but then I had a column our paper deemed worthy of publication and I was hooked. It was 1984, I was 65 years old and had a newfound passion that changed my life and continues to influence it to this day.

Since 1984, I have written many newspaper columns and feature stories, have had my work appear in nationally distributed magazines, and in 1998, when I was 79 years old, the first of my three books was published. Our sons adjusted well to their individual identities, one to become an attorney, the other a research/neuroscientist, and they live with their families thousands of miles apart—but their bond remains unique and strong. I think I have the best of all worlds. EMTNSTR

# ALONE AGAIN, NATURALLY

### · *Jeanne Aufmuth* ·

NATURALLY I'D HEARD THE BUZZ—the heartbreak, the emptiness, and the deep sense of loss that stem from a mother's essential life force and crowning glory vanishing onto an airplane to the East Coast or a fully loaded car headed to a Southern California college.

The eldest of my two daughters left for a Midwest university in the fall of 2001. Geographically undesirable as far as impromptu visits or attending that all-important sporting event. The transition wasn't terribly difficult, but it *was* a transition—an empty room, less sibling rivalry, and a change in family numbers that led to an altered (and dare I say improved?) family dynamic.

Perris, three years Waverley's junior, embraced her solo act with a vengeance, taking over dinner conversations and infusing the house with a bubbly, check-me-out spirit that was irresistible. Even the college application process was pleasurable with my youngest involved.

As high school graduation approached, lengthy conversations with empty-nester mom friends rose to a fevered pitch over multiple dinners and many more glasses of wine. How to walk away from a job that has defined most of your adult years? How to be all about yourself when it seems you've always been about others? How to re-kindle the flame with a man who has raised a family, not just the fire, with you for almost two decades?

For better or worse I am not one of those moms who existed solely for her children. I was a devoted soccer mom, chauffeur, cook, and classroom volunteer but am also a successful film critic, swordfighter, hockey player, and yogi. I assumed that I would work around the heartache of having Perris gone (also to the Midwest) by continuing with the activities I loved and facing new challenges. My Empty Nest Wish List looked something like this:

*Stripping/pole dancing* (NOTE TO SELF: PURCHASE SCANTY UNDERTHINGS)

*Hip-Hop lessons* (KRUMP AND JIVE TO THE CHILDLESS BEAT)

*Polish up my Spanish* (A TRAVESTY TO BE LESS THAN FLUENT IN CALIFORNIA)

*Singing group* (SHE KNOCKS DOWN WOMEN AND SMALL CHILDREN TO GET TO THE KARAOKE MACHINE)

*Learn ASL* (DO-GOODER SIGNS FOR THE HEARING IMPAIRED)

*Drawing/painting class* (STICK FIGURES BE GONE!)

*New York* (STILL HAVEN'T SEEN THE NEW MOMA)


A girl can dream...


*Contract killing* (IF GEENA DAVIS CAN DO IT SO CAN I)

*Fab view apartment in SF* (FINNISH INTERIORS)

*Take to the road with Stomp and become the penultimate Stomphead*

*Hop in the car sans props and* just keep driving

Much to my surprise, the heartache didn't materialize. When my husband and I dropped Perris at her dorm in Wisconsin my feeling wasn't of emptiness or sadness but of overwhelming pride: at the lovely daughter I had raised and the self-assured thrill that she was on the road to one of life's biggest and best adventures.

I've raised my girls to be communicators by being a communicator myself; that has tempered the sting of separation. We chat on an almost daily basis and I feel as involved in their lives as I did when they were living under my roof seven days a week. Boys, academics, alcohol, dorm-life—occasionally more than I want to know, but I definitely want to know it.

The transitions are different now. Visits home take on a life of their own that springs from the unbridled energies of two daughters, two stepdaughters, a 2-year-old granddaughter, and the complementary male companions. An excited anticipation segues into a kind of hyperactivity when my girls visit, involving the cooking of favorite foods, spirited conversations on a variety of noteworthy topics, and the ultimately not-so-unpleasant but eye-opening realization that we have adopted new and different routines to which we *all* relish a return.

As I approach this intriguing next phase, I am filled with a sense of freedom and childlike enthusiasm for the endless options I am afforded. I took up stripping and pole dancing in the fall, and aside from the daunting physical challenges, it's positively exhilarating to do something that's focused on a unique aspect of me.

Why has this emotionally loaded evolution not brought me to my knees? I ponder that often since many friends seem despondent at the loss of their kids. Don't get me wrong; I do have days when menopause and its snarky moods conspire to take me down. But if asked to offer advice on successful empty-nesting, I would boil it down to one essential philosophy: when you are your own woman (or man) confronting your interests and potential for adventure head-on, everyone wins: you for grabbing what life has to offer, your significant other for your ensuing happiness, and your children for a well-rounded and healthy role model who demonstrates peace of mind and an ease of balance. Not to mention killer pole skills!

I turned 50 recently (eek!), another inevitable step in the maturation process. My husband whisked me away to New York for a surprise celebration—cross MOMA off the list! An old friend gave me the gift of Flying Trapeze lessons and I took brush to paper today in my first watercolor class. I'm determined and excited to embrace all that life has to offer. Look out world, here I come! EMTNSTR

# Something to Leave Behind

· *Joanne Levy-Prewitt* ·

WHEN I WAS VERY SMALL, my grandmother rejoiced in seating me on a phone book at her dining room table behind her black Royal. Smiling as she read the poems and short stories I had hunted-and-pecked onto crisp typing paper, she said, "Maybe you'll be a writer one day." I used colored pencils to illustrate my creations, and proudly bound them in a folder that I still have today.

In my first years of college, inspired by a creative writing class, I wrote some short fiction and fantasized about a career as a fiction or screenwriter. I can't remember exactly why I stopped taking writing classes, but it might have had something to do with my growing student loan balance. Instead, I became a teacher, and by the time I became a mother I had neatly shelved my passion for writing.

Mothering became my creative outlet. I had created a child—a curious, bright, engaging child—and the rewards were enormous. With every day, every outing, and every conversation I was rewarded with the fruits of my labor, and it was enough—I didn't need the validation of the *Atlantic* or the *New Yorker* to know that

I had done something great—all I had to do was look across the dinner table each night.

But suddenly, and I do mean suddenly, my baby became a young man. A tall, fuzzy-faced, handsome young man. And one winter morning before high school, as he tucked his long legs underneath the breakfast table and inhaled three bowls of cereal, I realized he would leave. He would go off to college, and then to work, and someday he would start his own family. Yet, sad as I was to face life as something other than Matthew's Mother, part of me was very excited at the notion of returning to some of my own interests.

I was determined to make the most of his last few years at home. I took a leave of absence from teaching to do two things: work on my writing and savor every moment with my only child. As a teenager, Matt seemed to need me in new ways. After he started high school, he liked to stay up late at night to talk. At first, I thought he was looking for a way to avoid or postpone homework, but eventually it became clear that he wanted to talk about real things—friends, school, teachers, death, music, life. And since I no longer needed to wake up at 5:00 a.m. to get to my classroom, I stayed up and listened. It didn't take long to realize that what Matt needed, and what I wanted to give, was me.

During the day, I began writing fiction again. I took classes and joined several writing groups. I started a file; okay, two files, for my rejection letters. But I wrote. Writing gave me perspective, and the more I wrote the more I understood. With the creation of characters, I explored issues or people that confused me, and with the development of a plot, I controlled their fate. There was no question about my own fate, though; every time we discussed college, I felt impending doom.

Though writing fiction had become the best way to make sense of my world, whatever I wrote about my fears of being something other than a mother seemed horrible and trite—totally unreadable. But it was the process that helped ease the pain. Writing well is important to me, but sometimes, just writing, even if it's drivel, facilitates the truth. The truth was that I was afraid of losing the job I loved the most—afraid that the relationship I had cultivated with Matthew would dissolve— afraid that he'd no longer seek or need my advice—afraid that I wouldn't be important to anyone anymore.

\* \* \*

Letting go of Matthew wasn't easy. As he edged closer to high school graduation, some days, depressed and melancholy, my only solace was a stack of old home videos and a box of tissues. It was my way of letting go—revisiting the past and trying to imagine a new future—and the video footage provided all I needed to be reminded that the moments I spent raising Matthew were some of the best moments of my life. A naked infant sleeping on a sheepskin. A sweet preschooler wearing a paper bag lion mask. A confident teenager chanting Torah at his Bar Mitzvah. A tall man clutching his high school diploma.

His first year away was a blur. I wrote every day, and ramped up my career as an independent college adviser. My husband and I took a few short vacations strategically coordinated around Matt's trips home. On Sunday afternoons, Matt would often call, and again, while I thought he might be using me to postpone his studies, I loved hearing about his classes and friends.

Matt's been at college for nearly two years now, and I keep expecting to stop missing him, but I never do. There are mothers who rejoice in an empty house, but I miss the chaos. I miss the music—from the vulgar rap to the boom of Dvořák; I even miss the endless piles of laundry and orphaned socks. I miss the long after-dinner conversations about politics, religion, or comedy culminating with the consultation of the all-knowing Internet to settle a dispute. I miss the smell of a sweaty gym, or a muddy field, and the abundance of raw energy found at a music recital or school play. I miss late night musings and the baritone laughter of a small gathering of teenage boys far across the house. I miss the special way our dog barked to announce Matt's arrival up the front steps. I even miss the sound of the front door closing at three in the morning. I miss it all.

I wonder if my grandmother understood the link between parenting and writing. In both pursuits, whether conscious or not, I am creating something to leave behind. My grandmother's legacy is her wisdom—she let me know that I might leave more than children behind—I could leave my words. My life did not end when my son left for college. I have some sad moments—even sad days—when I am nostalgic for that sweet baby in my lap, but I'm also excited about what lies ahead—a happy, healthy adult son, travel and renewed closeness with my husband, and mornings spent at my keyboard.

The summer after Matt's freshman year in college, my first short story was published. It was a sweet moment—made all the sweeter that he was home to share it. I don't think children ever realize who we are other than parents. Maybe they're aware of some of our choices or sacrifices, but generally, I think they idealize us as fulfilled, strong adults. I wonder if Matthew understood the enormity and complexity of my tears the day I saw my own words in print—in raising him, I had already accomplished so much, but that day I realized that in many ways, I had left my mark. EMTNSTR

# REFEATHERING

## · Elizabeth Fishel ·

WHEN MY TWO SONS LEAVE for college, I drive around town in a heartsick daze as if after the breakup of a long, complicated affair. Every song on the car radio is "our" song. Each local landmark is one of "our" haunts steeped in memory and affection—the donut store where we braced ourselves after the earthquake; the ER where, five times, I paced and waited while the boys' sports injuries were sewn back together; the DMV where I dallied during their driving tests, and when my younger son passed, I looked so crestfallen the tester reassured me, "It's okay, he's a good driver."

Sometimes the gritty landscape where I raised Nate and Will rolls by in slow, sad motion, blurred by tears. But occasionally, a small shaft of internal sunlight pierces my gloom, and I'll allow myself to think, Hmm, what's next?

"I cried for three days when Sam left," says a friend who sent two daughters and a son off to college, "And then ..." The slow grin spreading across her face finishes her sentence and hints wordlessly at the x-rated parts.

A couple of weeks after my younger son departs, a close friend drops off an empty nest, a real one, at the door. Her kids are a bump older than mine, and a friend of hers gave her the nest when her children's leave-taking left her adrift. "Every unfinished separation from my own past came back to haunt me," is how she puts it. But five years later, she's reinventing her life in ways that give me hope. She knows it's my turn now, and she's passing along the nest to let me know that she's there for me and that good things will emerge to fill it.

Still, for those first few weeks after the boys are gone, the emptiness inside our house is almost palpable—the phone still, the rap music silenced, the zone from the front door to the kitchen hauntingly clutter-free. No soccer cleats, no soggy towels, no half-eaten burritos still in their take-out bags tumble across the floor. I'm haunted by a phrase that Nate coined in a seventh grade essay to describe the house before anyone else got home. A hollow watermelon, he called it, all the juicy parts gone. As I drift, rudderless, through the too-tidy, too-quiet rooms, I lust after that juicy red fruit, those messy seeds to spit all over the ground.

Part of me yearns to fill the space up quickly and noisily—adoption? a foreign student? importing someone from Telegraph Ave? "What are you going to do now?" my sister has asked me, almost pleading, at the end of the summer before. We've raised our two sets of sons on parallel tracks and shared every sweetness and stumble. She's five years younger, and sometimes my life is the writing on her wall, the tea leaves for her own future. "I have no idea," I answer, and then feigning more confidence than I feel, I add, "But things will evolve."

The tiny nest, even empty, is cozy and snugly put together with fuzzy bits of this and that and a scratchy few strands breaking off in no particular direction. Inside, my friend has tucked a flamingo-pink plastic egg and a note that reads, "It's a love nest, of course."

For years I've heard people say that waving grown children off to college can be an unnerving moment of reckoning in a marriage. Will we still like each other after all those years of sweeping things under the rug to get on with family life? Will we have things to talk about when it's just us two without childish interruptions and the protective din of their uproar? How will we shape the calendar without the seasons easing seamlessly from soccer to basketball to baseball and tennis? Indeed, this fork in the road seems littered with marital casualties. There's the husband we know who announced that after the couple's two daughters were gone, he was going, too. I imagine he was startled when his wife didn't stop him. Apparently, she felt the same way.

"I worried about my dad all alone in our big, empty house," said one of our son's friends who'd left for college soon after her parents divorced. "But he did all right. He got a lot closer to my cat." Yes, it's amazing how adaptable we two-legged creatures can be.

So setting just two places at the dinner table, Bob and I start to adjust and settle in. Dinner can be stylishly late with no ravenous sons home from practice, chomping at the bit, ready to devour the house. Meals can be random and casual and leftovers cobbled together without complaints. In the serene silence that settles over the dinner hour—no ringing cell phones or vibrating text messages—I learn a strange thing—my husband is rather chatty. He hasn't gotten a word in for two decades, and by now, he's saved up a few stories. He basks in the undivided attention and gives it back.

We can pad around naked upstairs and jump into bed without keeping an ear out for basketballs bouncing down the street, the sign for years that our sons were home from the park. We can also leave town at the drop of a hat. Weekend overnights used to require preparations to equal the invasion of Normandy, so for twenty-five years we went away only once a year—on our anniversary. Now we dash off whenever the spirit moves us—a romantic B & B, a mountain cabin, a spiritual retreat to gaze at each other's navels, if not our own.

Though loving, even craving this gallivanting, I've always been something of a homebody, a cocooner even before the type was named—besides childraising, I've also spent decades writing books and articles, leading writers' groups, and organizing projects at home. Now, I find myself in a flurry of nesting unlike anything I've experienced since I got ready for my babies' births.

Back then I was in and out of baby stores like a mother bear on the prowl, hunting for the sturdy crib, the soft, tiny-flower patterned bolsters and blankets, the wicker changing table borrowed from a friend, the musical mobile and handmade quilts I'd hang just so.

Often at night I'd wander into my babies' pristinely empty but soon-to-be-bustling nurseries, settle into their rocking chairs, and dream not only of my yet-to-be-born children but also of the mother I was about to become. Furnishing their rooms became the first step to imagining a new life-stage into being.

Now I'm birthing another era, decorating another interior. The imagery has changed, but the intensity and the pleasure of it feel somehow familiar. This time I'm in and out of lighting stores, brightening up moody corners of our house with artful lamps. At the same time, I'm tearing down funky old shades and curtains and ordering new ones, soft and stylish ones for warmth and privacy and an uptick of color.

But it's in my study that I take my strongest stand, getting ready for new possibilities to take root. I lobbied for this room when we moved into the house five years ago. Because we burrowed through a walled-off closet and down a narrow set of stairs to reach this wide-windowed, sunlit-filled, garden-gazing space, I dubbed it Narnia, knowing it could become the magic wardrobe of my imagination. The boys, then teen-agers, eyed it, too, because its private entrance would have been perfect for late-night sneaks, either in or out. But I held firm, knowing my sons would need this space only in passing, while I was putting down stakes for the long haul.

Yet once I claimed the room and filled it with desk, computer, and towering piles of files, it felt functional but soulless, not yet a room of my own. The shared rooms in the house demanded attention; leaky sinks, buckling tile, sagging sofas had to be fixed up first. But now I see that our emptied-out home has become a gift of time and freed-up inner space to re-feather my own nest. I'm ready to add my totems of inspiration, my signposts to the territory ahead. I bring home a kilim rug patterned in earthy rusts and terra cottas and a range of blues from turquoise to teal. It grounds my room yet gives it poetry and a color scheme. I pick out baskets to hide those towering files and an aqua-shaded lamp with the body of a ceramic horse that bathes my desk in mellow light. I reupholster my somber-grey, downer of a desk chair in a shocking swathe of inspiring indigo blue and add a back pillow from my sons whose colors make a soulful harmony together. Finally, beside my desk, I hang a multitiered, turquoise painted shelf, exactly the color of my childhood room, and fill it with my newly expanding collection of global dolls. I had such a collection as a child and am reinventing it now, doll by doll—a Yucatan mother with bambinos on her back, a Bermudan woman in bright batiks, a taffeta-skirted Greek folk dancer—mementos of the places I've been and where I dream of heading.

If the house is a symbol of the self, my season of nesting has been a face-lift without the pain of a nip and tuck. I'm emerging from it refreshed and energized but missing the telltale strain around the eyes, the smile that doesn't quite relax. Light and shade, warmth and privacy, splashes of color and bursts of whimsy—into this space will come my stories yet to be written, my adventurous tales yet to be told.

Still, I'm leaving the front door ajar. My latest domestic purchase caused the usual eyebrow raise from my husband. "What do we need that for?" he asked as he saw me plumping the cushions on a plushy new chair I was making comfortable in the corner of our bedroom. He knows we both enjoy reading propped up on pillows in bed. "Oh, this is just in case one of the boys is home and needs a place to sit and talk with us," I toss over my shoulder, just as casual as I can be. ▪

PART TWO

# LEAVING ON A JET PLANE

# READY OR NOT

## · *Marilyn O'Malley* ·

I WAS A BUDDING YOUNG FEMINIST with a million plans and a huge birth control failure. I wasn't yet 21, and there he was in my belly—it was not one of my plans.

I sensed the moment of his conception and his urge to be born. I was not particularly spiritual, but I knew what I felt. The experience spoke for itself, against reason, against all those plans that I had ... and definitely against my conviction never to have children.

His voice shouted out from that dark, mysterious place, "Ready or not, Mom, here I come!"

True to that prenatal bravado, Joe was born a healthy, spunky, incredibly present little creature with broad shoulders and a loud, demanding cry. The first time he walked, he swaggered: chest out and head held high, a loud gutsy grunt asserting his existence.

"He's all boy!" strangers commented approvingly. Joe looked everybody straight in the eye and bellowed joyful recognition as if they had met before. At first I cringed. I had an agenda to prove that sexual stereotypes were the product of societal expectations. I dressed him in all kinds of colors, not just little boy blue. I put dolls in his crib. I let his hair grow in lovely golden curls that framed his pink cheeks and bright eyes. And still he was "all boy" to everyone.

Another voice came from within: *"Let him be who he is."* I relaxed and let my son unfold himself.

*   *   *

Joe was sensitive and liked pretty things, but beyond that he was a whirlwind. He was coordinated and strong from the very beginning, excelling at any physical task he took on, and never very interested in sitting still.

He understood instinctively that it was cruel to pull the cat's tail, and ran over and pushed down a little girl who did, yelling "No owie kitty! No owie kitty!" He was on a mission to protect the weak before he could even speak properly.

Joe and I grew up together. Through days of meager paychecks, we survived on beans and rice. Despite my sometimes awkward personal life, we persevered. No matter what happened, there was always the two of us. Joe and me.

Despite the lack of a steady male role model, Joe grew up with good values about hard work, fairness, and honesty. He set goals. He had a natural ability to read people, often denouncing my dates as "scumbags" or "losers" and I would have done well to listen.

Puberty hit with an ornery streak that often landed him in the principal's office. I struggled through his adolescence as much as he did, having to promise to stop his backtalk, while wondering how I could possibly control a kid who could lift me into the air, outrun, out-shout, and often outsmart me. Fortunately, he loved his mom and didn't really want to see me hauled away, so he settled down by the beginning of high school.

Sometimes I complained that his goals were never academic, but I was proud when he earned letters in baseball and soccer, and when he conducted the school orchestra. Counselors told me it was fortunate he had music and sports because they'd hate to think how that wild energy might otherwise manifest.

He stopped a knife fight in the locker room at school. One kid pulled a knife on another kid, and Joe jumped across the bench, wrestled him down, and took the knife. I had no reason to doubt the tale. I'd seen his fearlessness and his friends often recounted stories of Joe's bravery in protecting others. A mixture of fear and pride and relief welled up in me. Sometimes I wished he wasn't so fearless.

My son graduated in one piece, and with many friends. He was voted "Most Spirited Senior" and posed for the yearbook in a girl's cheerleading outfit, grinning unabashedly from ear to ear. The future before him seemed uncertain, though. His grades weren't going to do much for him.

I guess it stood to reason that Joe would join the service, especially since I'd been trying his whole life to discourage it. My parents had both served and so had many relatives and ancestors. It was a predictable direction for a young man who didn't like sitting still, could fight for a soccer ball like he was possessed, and had the courage to jump in and protect others with his life.

*"Let him be who he is."* This time the voice could not calm me.

My heart raced. My head spun. My only child. I had grown up in this military family and knew the stories. It horrified me. *"Ready or not, Mom, here I go."*

Friends and relatives gave me platitudes. It would be good for him. It would teach him discipline. What was the likelihood that he would ever actually be in combat? And even if he did see action, the odds were in his favor that he would survive, they said. I wept. I knew he would go to war, just the way I knew the moment he was conceived. I tried to console myself with the statistics about the likelihood of his survival.

There was nothing I could do. He was 18 and he'd already signed the papers. The recruiters had stolen my son from behind my back. I felt betrayed and stricken. I was sick at heart and reeling with grief and fear.

I wept some more. I had no control over his fate. The only thing I could do was give him my support and send him off with fervent prayers. I was proud that he had the courage and conviction to do what he believed was right, even if I did not agree, so I tried to honor that instead of focus on my anguish.

Weeks went by and I stood in the door of his room and mourned daily. Where was my baby? What were they doing to him? I felt helpless and overwhelmed.

Then there was just plain missing him, regardless of where he was or why he had gone. The times I had yelled at him not to slam the door or not to be so loud haunted me. How I wanted to hear that door slam and the walls rattle! To hear that boisterous voice shout, "Hi Mom! I'm home!"

I wanted to throw my arms around his brawny shoulders and pull him to me, smell the sweat in his hair mingled with too much aftershave ... to feel his heart beat and his chest rise and fall. Gone from my arms, from my home, from my protection.

I counted out the weeks until he would return and then it hit me that he would not be returning to stay. He would only return for a short while. Never again would we live under the same roof, except maybe years from now when I am elderly. My world was changed forever. My baby had left home. *Ready or not....*

\*       \*       \*

My son survived combat several times. I endured years of agonizing worry, and somehow managed not to die myself before he finally returned to civilian life after nine years of serving our country. A mixture of pride, fear, and relief still well up in me when I think of what he's been through. I still get tears in my eyes sometimes when I remember slamming doors and a loud voice announcing his arrival.

But some wonderful days he comes to my house to visit, and to my great joy, he still makes a boisterous entry. EMTNSTR

# BLUE SKY

## · Roque Gutierrez·

THE SUN DANCED in the blue, blue sky the day my son Xavier sailed away on board the USS Mt. Vernon. My wife and I, my son's fiancée, and her entire family stood on the pier waving like we were in an insurance commercial as the huge troop ship sailed away. Then we all jumped in our cars and raced across the Coronado Bridge connecting Coronado Island to San Diego. We dashed through a park and onto the beach, and did more waving as the ship passed the island. We couldn't be sure if Xavier saw us. He never mentioned it.

All of us were upset at this latest development in my son's life, but he had decided to join the Marines because he couldn't find work. That he didn't find it an honorable thing to do as much as a desperate one, didn't sit so well with us. But at the age of 24 and several years out of high school with limited college, we accepted his assurance that everything would be okay. Then, of course, the war started.

No one told us the part about having to sit around for months wondering where in the world he was and dreading all knocks on the door and any evening phone calls. There weren't any guide-books to see us through. It wasn't like he had gone off to college or anything like that. Did I mention camp?

Suffice it to say that men-children aren't the most reliable when it comes to keeping in touch, so when we did hear from him the nonchalance in his voice made me want to come through the phone on more than one occasion. After all, we were shedding tears and wringing the skin off our hands sitting in front of the TV every evening watching the latest developments in a war nei-ther of us supported. But we loved our son and loved our boys over there and so we zipped our lips and waited.

The days were bad enough, but the nights were insufferable. It was when we did most of our crying. We would hold each other for support and wake up the next morning, with neither of us feeling that we had gotten any rest. The lines on our faces deepened, as did our concern for our son.

\*     \*     \*

It's a funny thing about waiting; the end is never like the be-ginning. What I mean is that, as time wore on, and the nearer my son came to coming home, our fears seemed to grow. It was the worst nightmare that we could conceive of: that he would be on the brink of coming home when some tragedy would strike and we would lose him. Our hearts ached to be near him now more than ever, to make sure he made it that last mile, or thou-sand miles.

The day he returned we were all lined up again, only this time our other children were there too; it appeared as though a rock star was coming home, and in a way, it was true—only he was our rock star, our son Xavier.

Now we were sure the hard part was just beginning. We assumed that he would suffer postwar shock or exhibit some distressing symptoms from the sudden return home. While he did suffer some of these things to a lesser and greater degree, his most telling change was his ability to accept and overcome challenges, something he had a hard time coping with before his trip overseas.

So we were lucky, we got our son back and he had become a man. But looking back on it now, I would never trade the boy for war; not now, not ever. EMTNSTR

# Missing Matthew

· *Laura Shumaker* ·

MY FOURTEEN-YEAR-OLD SON ANDY skipped ahead of me with his fresh haircut and his new Quicksilver T-shirt and tumbled into a cluster of exuberant but nervous freshmen outside the high school gym as upperclassmen clapped and chanted, music blaring. It was orientation day at our local high school.

When it was time to get to the business of filling out forms and taking pictures for student body cards, I felt a tug on my sleeve. It was the choral teacher, who had taught my sixteen-year-old son the previous year.

"I hear you sent Matthew away to school," he said coldly.

"Yeah, it's tough, but I think it will be good for him in the long run."

"Well, I think it's sad," he said, then turned and walked away.

I raced around and paid for books and registration fees with Andy running behind me, knowing I was distressed. I kept my chin to my chest, my eyes down. Only a few of my good friends could tell that something was wrong as tears stained my beet red face and my light blue T-shirt. "I'm fine," I lied to Andy with my best fake smile. "Go ahead and talk to your friends. I'll meet you in the car." I ran to the car, the goofy smile still planted on my face, fell in, and sobbed for what felt like a long time. It was the first time I had cried since leaving Matthew, who is autistic, at Camphill Special School, three thousand miles away, near Philadelphia, just two days before. Andy was right behind me, and sat next to me as I wept, patting my back lightly and giving me sips from his water bottle.

"You did the right thing, Mom," he said, "That teacher wouldn't have said that if he knew what we've been through."

And indeed, we had been through a lot as a family, though the last year had been particularly difficult. Matthew is what many would consider high-functioning, but his quirky and impulsive behavior that had been manageable in earlier years had become unwieldy and even dangerous with the onslaught of adolescence. There were rages, slamming doors, and police visits prompted by Matthew's knack for approaching strangers, mostly young, prepubescent girls and their mothers, with inappropriate questions.

"How old are you? Do you think I'm nice? Can I touch your hair?"

A series of disturbing close calls was topped off with a surprise letter from an attorney. Apparently, Matthew had collided with his client, a young boy, while riding his bike.

"Matthew? Were you in a bicycle accident? Was anyone hurt?"

"Probably a boy. Who told you?"

My husband and I came to the heartbreaking conclusion that

Matthew was no longer safe in the community where he had grown up, and that his impulsive actions were putting others in peril. He needed more supervision, more than we or our local school could provide.

I wasn't prepared for the way I felt when my husband and I returned after taking Matthew to Pennsylvania. I had assumed that I could finally enjoy the luxury of time alone at home with Matthew well taken care of and the other boys at school. I imagined I would reconnect with friends over lunch and at the gym. The strain that had aged my face would fall away, and I would look and feel rested and serene.

But instead, I felt scattered and aimless. The toll of the anxious summer drained me of energy and confidence, and my identity felt battered. I had been the Matthew expert for fifteen years. I had known exactly how to hold him when he fussed as a baby, and I knew the story behind every scar and broken bone. I was the only one who knew how to calm him down during an adolescent, autistic meltdown. But now I felt I had been stripped of my duties.

I didn't dare share my despair with friends, family, or even my husband. They would throw up their hands and say, "But this is what you wanted! Stop whining!" It seemed selfish to fill the time Matthew's absence granted me with luxurious activities such as seeing friends for lunch, relaxing in the garden, or even doing a load of laundry without interruption.

After a few weeks, when I was considering kicking myself in gear and venturing out to the grocery store, the phone rang. It was one of my more clueless friends.

"Has Matthew left yet? Good! You must be so relieved! He doesn't come home till Thanksgiving? *Thank God!*"

Her insensitivity fueled me with anger, and after hanging up on her, I went into a housecleaning frenzy until Andy reminded me it was time to leave for freshman orientation.

*　　*　　*

After Andy and I returned from the scene of my public breakdown, I picked up where I left off with the housecleaning frenzy, though with less steam. When I turned off the vacuum, I heard the phone ring and rushed to get it.

"Hello, Laura? This is Andrea at Camphill."

Andrea was Matthew's housemother.

"Things are going well here, but I have some questions about Matthew, and I hope you can help me." My heart jumped. *Yes! I can help! What do you need to know?*

"What are his favorite foods?" she asked. "Does he like music? How do you reward him for good behavior? He has been teasing his roommate relentlessly."

*That's a good sign. At least I know he's feeling like himself.*

"Any ideas? The rash that was on his hands seems to have cleared up since you left, and he is sleeping well. We are enjoying him so much!" Andrea told me that Matthew liked to watch her son Joe, who was 18, work in the greenhouse, and that they got along well.

I felt overwhelmed with joy and relief. Matthew was still far away, but he was safe, he was happy, and he was appreciated.

We talked for almost a half hour, mother to mother, and I told her to call me *any*time. It occurred to me that I had felt that I was a failure as a mother, because I couldn't fix Matthew. But now Andrea was acknowledging that Matthew was a puzzle, and that we needed each other to figure him out and help him grow.

"May I say hello to Matthew?"

"He's right here."

"Hi, Matthew!"

"Hi, Mom. I'm very busy right now. Joe and I are doing something very important."

"I know. I just wanted to hear your voice." I said, choking up. "I miss you, Matthew, and I love you *so* much."

I could tell he was smiling.

"That's nice." EMTNSTR

# OUT IN THE WORLD
# (AND BARELY A WORD)

### · John Leland ·

WHEN WE TOLD FRIENDS that our son, Jordan, would not go right to college after finishing high school last year, but would instead teach English in rural Kenya, the reactions were supportive but somehow not to the point.

"That'll be a life-changing experience for him," they said.

"I wish I'd done that when I was 18," they said.

"He'll be so much more ready for college when he goes," they said.

We were familiar with the sentiments. We had spent the previous year encouraging Jordan not to leap automatically into college. And we knew the benefits. If he didn't get malaria, dengue fever, Rift Valley fever, or other diseases; if he didn't lose his passport (again); if the war between neighboring Ethiopia and Somalia didn't splash over to his village; if he didn't drink the water; if he didn't under any circumstances have unprotected sex, then this was certainly the best thing for him.

What was missing from our friends' best wishes was a sense of priorities. Sure, the gap year was good for Jordan. But what about us?

Here we were, three weeks after dropping him off in Nairobi—and two weeks after the latest deadly carjacking of Americans in the city—and we had no word from him, little faith in the program organizers, and no means to reach him except by e-mail, knowing that he was in some village (we knew not which) without electricity, let alone Internet access. The State Department web site warned travelers to Kenya that, "violent criminal attacks, including armed carjacking and home invasions/burglary, can occur at any time and in any location, and are becoming increasingly frequent, brazen, vicious and often fatal."

Fat chance I'd be getting a school hoodie and N.C.A.A. tickets out of this plan.

While other parents could cite the brand of air conditioner in their child's dorm room, all we knew was that—presuming things had gone according to plan—Jordan was somewhere in the 539-square-mile Kakamega District, being called on to do things no living human being had ever seen him do, such as run a secondary-school classroom or try unfamiliar foods.

American colleges and universities have turned the parental experience into a magnificently catered consumer banquet, with slick promotional literature, introductory weekends, testimonials from satisfied customers, and backward-walking sales staff, even too-cozy tie-ins with loan providers. The colleges function not so much in loco parentis as in loco concierge.

The gap year had none of that. It was an exercise in improvisation, guesswork, and information deprivation.

Counselors at Jordan's private high school, who were so resourceful with advice about colleges, drew a blank when we asked about gap-year options. Though colleges widely recommend a gap year, high school counselors are still judged, like their schools, by what colleges graduates get into. They suggested we look online. And good luck.

A Google search turned up commercial agencies, like Dynamy and whereyouheaded.com that promised, for a fee, to design the perfect program. We dismissed these out of hand. It was one thing to pay thousands of dollars for your teenager to volunteer in a poor rural village, but another to pay someone to customize the poverty experience.

After some searching online, Jordan selected a teaching internship in Ghana, run by a Massachusetts-based nonprofit organization called Global Routes. Ghana seemed a perfect destination: far removed from the biosphere of New York private schools, yet safe and predictable.

Behind the web site, Global Routes turned out to be something of a black box; you didn't know what you were getting until you were in it. Shortly after Jordan committed to the Ghana program, the organization informed him that it might go to India or Kenya instead—they'd let him know. Even after they decided on Kenya (about five weeks before the start date), they told us not to contact the in-country group leader for information.

So we were sending our only son, 18, halfway around the world to a country he hadn't chosen. The organizers couldn't tell us the name of the hotel where the group of five students would start or the village where they would work, and we couldn't contact the leader who would be a lifeline if anything went wrong.

We swallowed hard but went ahead. The point of a gap year, after all, was to encounter the unknown, and here it was. Before Jordan left, a friend's son was hospitalized after an asthma attack in a dorm in Brooklyn, a few miles from his home. Danger, we realized, was not "over there" but wherever your child could find it.

The cost was about $6,000 for three months, including room and board with a host family and periodic travel throughout the country. The University of Wisconsin, which had deferred Jordan's admission until the next September, would not give credit for the internship. But six grand for a semester-long learning experience, even if you add airfare and $1,400 worth of injections (insurance didn't pay a dime), was less expensive than a semester at most colleges, and we hoped it would prepare him pedagogically for the pillars of American higher ed, beer pong, and freshman comp.

For us, the hard part was the silence. Jordan had traveled outside the all-reaching tentacles of high-tech parenting, and we were suddenly in an info-vacuum. We sent e-mail messages into the ether and began each day looking for a response. We turned into the insufferable New York parents who natter compulsively about their children, a stereotype we had avoided. And at home we worried, in part because we didn't know what to worry about.

Four weeks into his teaching internship, Jordan finally sent us an e-mail from an Internet cafe in Kakamega. All was well. He described his new family of siblings and his "mother," a 70-year-old materfamilias who doted on him and always wanted him to eat more (we loved her already). His village, it turns out, was called Shichinji. We'd given him way too much insect repellent. We settled into the position of college parents everywhere, who accept long silences broken only by pleas for money (in Jordan's case, donations toward an independent project, buying textbooks for his impoverished school).

In April he emerged from a ramp at Newark airport, tan and healthy-looking, sneakers ragged and hair long. He spent the next weeks glued to his computer and DVDs—if he was a changed man, he was keeping it to himself.

For us, the lessons of the gap year include newfound confidence in our son and an intimate knowledge of just how much it costs to call a cell phone in Africa.

As for what Jordan got out of the gap year, you'll have to ask him yourself. We've tried, to little avail. At the end, he is still an eighteen-year-old: opaque, independent, more resistant to parental curiosity than responsive to it.

Like our friends, I wish I had taken a gap year when I was Jordan's age. I'm sure it would have been a life-changing experience. But I realize now that you would have to be an eighteen-year-old to understand the changes. At that age, after all, maturation isn't a goal; it's the current you swim in. But at least when he encounters beer pong and freshman comp—and opportunity and disappointment—he'll be able to draw on his successes in a world where none of those things can be taken for granted.

And someday, perhaps, he'll cough up the school hoodie and N.C.A.A. tickets. EMTNSTR

# THE BIG UNEASY

*Philip Weingrow*

I THOUGHT IT WAS going to be easy. Jake moved out of our home, but not far away. He was in his early 20s. He started working, got his own place. Later he moved in with his girlfriend, but still came by for dinners and events; an expanding extended family...very old school.

Shortly after Jake moved out, my wife had a terrible time when her eighteen-year-old daughter moved 3,000 miles away to go to school. It was very painful to witness my wife trying to adjust to not having her daughter around and the great feelings of loss that went with it. The fact that she supported her daughter's decision and knew it was coming did little to make it easier. I felt fortunate not to have to go through that painful separation. Then, inevitably perhaps, things changed.

"Dad, we broke up. We tried hard to make it work. It just wasn't happening. I feel real sad. I don't know what to do."

Children can't understand how the pain they feel transmits over the phone lines right into a parent's heart, then stays there longer than it does with the child. (Probably because our children tend not to tell us when they're feeling better ... rotten kids!)

*  *  *

Weeks passed, and then the other shoe dropped. "Dad, I'm thinking of moving to New York. I think this would be a good time for me to do what I really want to do and try to make it in the music industry. New York's the place to be."

New York! My son, my baby! In that big, cruel, crime-ridden, hustling city? What is he, crazy? How can he survive there? Look, I grew up in New York. I know all about that place. I scream all of this inside my head as I say, "That sounds very exciting Jake!" ("What are you, crazy?!?" I'm still screaming.)

"Do you have any friends there? Do you know anyone in the industry?"

"No, I don't," he responds calmly. "But I've been doing a lot of research online. I've been sending my resume and looking at neighborhoods and want to check it out."

I think of the loneliness. I think of how easy it is to be taken advantage of in my hometown. I think a million things that have more to do with me than him. I worry.

I'm told that men don't often acknowledge their worries. Their wives, mothers, and girlfriends know they worry. But they won't acknowledge it to themselves. It's way too scary. It symbolizes a loss of control. Little is scarier to a man than that.

"I don't want to feel these things, damn it! I want to fix it!" I hear myself scream. (Paradoxically, I have to listen to myself real carefully to know when I'm screaming inside. Why? I think I'm in too much of a state of panic to notice.)

In not acknowledging my worries, my loss of control, I have learned that I can't begin to understand this sense of loss I feel. But that I learn later. Right now: I want to find him a place to live. I want to help him get a job. Who do I still know who can help him? Where can I get some information that would be useful? Who can look after him for me?

My God! I drive myself crazy with my inability to fix this thing. This thing, of course, is my worry; my worries and my desire to get control of them. For though there is a grown man standing before me, fully equipped and capable, I can't see this. I see my child; my young, needy, adorable, clever child.

*   *   *

In the days that follow, my wife, Jake's stepmother, consoles me. It dawns on me for the first time that three years earlier, when she sent her daughter off to the same city to go to college, I didn't get it at all.

Oh sure, I understood that she would miss her bright, fun-loving daughter. But I didn't get it like I did when I was losing my son. And that's the way it felt: like I was losing a part of myself. I don't know how anyone can understand what that means without having the experience. And it is an experience parents all need to have. It is the other part of our child's need to separate, because, after all, they are different, separate people from their parents. But while we act that way on the surface, deep down, something more primitive and visceral goes on.

This attachment to our children, and they to us, has been

crafted over approximately two decades of almost daily inter-twining of our lives. We become part of each other. They learn what buttons to push and who we are, even the parts we don't want them to know. They become so obvious to us. We know "that look" and what's coming next. What we rarely examine, however, is the effect we have on each other. It usually takes an event to make us stop and wonder. Our children leaving home is such an event.

Parents are often amazed that their children are well-behaved with others, or that they eat spinach. They have learned from us, even if they don't want to show us. Why? So they can be themselves ... a part of the separation process. How in hell we accomplish the separation at all is still a big mystery to me!

*　　*　　*

So here is the good part:

A week or so later, I took Jake to the airport. We never seemed closer. My son, who had never been far from home, was extraor-dinarily brave—much more so than his old man. We gave each other one long hug (I feared it might be our last) and he went off. I cried so hard I could barely see well enough to drive.

As I write this, it is the one-month anniversary of his de-parture. Jake has found an apartment in Brooklyn, with room-mates he located online. He got a job, which he also found online (nothing old school about Jake) with a Grammy award-winning recording studio in Manhattan.

Because I know now how capable Jake is, I worry a whole lot less. I'm also very proud. There is now enough calmness inside (the screaming has stopped ... about this) that I can consider the connections between Jake and me. It occurs to me that I left New York at the age of 25 to come to California, with no job, no place to live, and little cash in my jeans. Jake went to New York at the age of 27 under similar circumstances. We both left our respective homes in the same month. We both wanted to start new. We both wanted some adventure. I don't believe these are coincidences. To me, it speaks to how our lives are intertwined. It can make the pain great, but recognizing the connections permits me to understand the benefits.

Fortunately for Jake, as well as for me, he would have none of my feeble attempts to help him out. He had a strong desire to do this on his own. He was both determined and brave. In this way, he has already succeeded. He has successfully made a significant step in separating and becoming his own person.

I'm glad I had the good sense to back off and he had the good sense to keep me at bay. [EMTNSTR]

Part Three

# DOWN TO ONE

# RITE OF PASSAGE DAY

### · *Sharon Rockey* ·

I DIDN'T KNOW WHAT HAD BECOME of the sweet little pre-teen-
ager who had once read me to sleep from the *Tao of Pooh*. She
never knew how grateful I'd been to hear her innocent voice
reading those comforting passages—words that drifted into
the night air and dissolved into silent tears. Being a single
mom was a harsh reality for both of us, and most of the time
I wasn't sure I could hold it together.

She would suffer through long hours of my being away at work
and the weeks of study as I struggled to pass the Securities Exam.
I barked at her for expecting me to stop and help her with her
homework, until that evening she came and pulled me away from
the books into the living room, turned on the stereo and made
me dance. As the music washed over me and we spun around the
room laughing, it was as if I was experiencing physical sensations
for the very first time. She was only 14. Where had she learned
this magic?

And now she was leaving for college ... and ... she was angry.
Who could blame her? I'd been so caught up in my new career,

she'd gotten lost in the shuffle somewhere during those precious high school years. But I wouldn't have known how to be there for her even if I had realized the depth of her unhappiness, nor was I fully aware of the huge disconnect between us. Feeling proud of a child and bragging to your friends does not a good mom make.

As the time grew near, my anxiety over her leaving was made all the more heart-wrenching by our inability to communicate. Finally, I made a desperate and radical suggestion, something completely foreign to both of us—we scheduled an appointment with a therapist.

It wasn't as if I expected a therapist to undo the damage that had been years in the making. But I sensed that my daughter had a lot that needed to be said before she left, and whatever it was, she wasn't saying it to me.

For most of the hour, we sat looking straight ahead at the therapist, rarely glancing at one another. She spoke, I replied; I spoke, she replied. The therapist was amazed at her honesty and how articulately she expressed herself, how well reasoned her conclusions were. It was obvious that this young woman understood how my acts of omission and commission had affected her life. Her words were ruthlessly painful for me, but cathartic at the same time.

I wanted to believe that the session had offered something of value for her. I knew it had for me. The therapist asked us to make this pact: I would promise to take a whole day off from my job and celebrate it with her. My daughter would choose three things she wanted us to do and at the end of the day each of us would present the other with a gift we had made ourselves—something that would represent our Rite of Passage Day together.

We set a date a few weeks out and started thinking about what to make. I was stunned to discover how difficult it was to keep my end of the bargain. The ideas kept getting pushed aside by immediate projects at work. At one point, the whole ritual day plan had become so faint in my mind, that I found myself entertaining thoughts of just forgetting the whole thing.

That really scared me! Here it was thrown right in my face—all the reasons that had led up to the pact in the first place, coming up to be reckoned with. What was wrong with me? What WAS important to me? It was then that I got serious and devoted all my evenings for the next couple of weeks to working on my gift.

I found a small wooden box and began to collage it with photos and words cut from magazines. The top of the lid would represent her new freedom, a young woman in full blossom, off to discover the limitless world. The underside of the lid represented her spirituality, her gifts of perception, and symbols to remind her to keep following her own inner guidance. The bottom had snippets from her childhood, images from her favorite books, and silly jokes we had shared. Inside were decorated envelopes with special mementos that only had meaning for the two of us. The therapist must have known that the very act of creating the gift would have far more significance to me than the gift itself. And even though I couldn't fool myself into thinking that this one gesture could make up for so much that had been lost, it was important to me that I'd kept my promise and I wanted this to be a special day.

I picked her up and we headed for the first place on her list, a hip little café in Sausalito that I'd never even heard of. I felt awkward sitting there with her, but the rest of the day unfolded as if someone had been running a few steps ahead making sure everything was perfect. Next stop was the San Francisco Museum of Modern Art. I hated driving in the city. I get confused, she loses patience, and parking is next to impossible. It felt risky, but I drove straight to a parking spot that miraculously appeared a block away.

The art was exciting—so far so good—and then it was off to the exhibit hall at the California Academy of Sciences adjacent to Golden Gate Park, where we would later picnic by the lagoon and exchange our gifts. Not only was there a parking place right at the main entrance of the hall, I gasped when I saw the huge banner above the door, "Rites of Passage From Around the World." What kind of magic was this?

No one could have planned what was about to happen next. Inside the hall, we were introduced to a modern-day medicine man from Nigeria. Right on the spot he offered to give my daughter her own personalized rite of passage ceremony. He gathered some of his friends around as witnesses, then poured water through her hair, recited some poetic incantations intended to cut the ties of the past, and ended with wishes for good fortune on her journey into the next phase of her life. Afterwards, as we made our way to the lagoon, there were no words to describe what had just happened.

We exchanged gifts. She'd made a cutout drawing of herself with elfish ears and feet. She was naked, straddling the globe against a starry sky, and waving farewell. The picture said it all, "I am independent, I am unashamed, accept me as I am, I am free to be me."

The day ended with us sitting there by the lagoon and me thinking aloud, "The only thing left to make this day complete, is for someone to come along and take our picture."

She was still angry when she left for school. But she's experienced many of her own Rites of Passage since our day in the park. She's moved to another country, and she's married with two beautiful children. She's still a creative, intelligent, and highly perceptive woman and ... she still has her little collaged box. But she stayed angry with me for many years until, by some mysterious grace, a new understanding grew between us. Maturity changes people. And now as I sit here admiring that photo taken by the stranger in the park so long ago, I embrace her forgiveness as the most welcome and blessed Rite of Passage in my life. EMTNSTR

# THE PROPERTIES OF PARADISE

· *Ransom Stephens* ·

THERE ARE NO HALF-FULL PEPSI CANS on the coffee table and I didn't trip over her backpack when I got up to answer the phone and it wasn't a teenager at the other end, it was some idiot trying to sell me a vacation to paradise. It sounds stupid, but hunting for the TV remote is comforting. I almost hope I don't find it so I can call her and blame her for losing it. It doesn't really matter though, I don't know what channel the dumb show she used to watch is on anyway. I don't know what CD has my favorite song either. Maybe I'll call her anyway.

The reality of a clean house with Van Morrison at half-volume isn't how I pictured it last weekend. The house was a mess while she packed. And Marilyn Manson was grating on my nerves at full volume. It was wonderful. It's not just the quiet that I can't stand. It's the lack of dirty socks in the living room, the lack of teenagers rushing in and out the door, and there aren't any moldy coffee mugs in strange places. I don't know what it is, but I miss it.

\*   \*   \*

We traveled a tough road after her mom moved away. I resisted the urge to drag her home to California, enough in her life had changed and I couldn't rationalize changing our geography and culture, too. So, like two fish in a foreign ocean, we stayed in Texas. I don't think there was a warmer home than the one we made together in that funny looking A-frame house in that little valley between Dallas and Fort Worth that flooded every spring. Nothing in our life there was normal. There's just no manual for a single father raising an adolescent daughter. Middle school was the worst. It seemed like every damn problem known to the adolescent girl culture haunted us—body image, cutting, hair pulling, the whole Gothic underground, not to mention sex, drugs, and rock and roll. I learned the discipline to shut up and let her earn my trust, and she played her flute, argued with the Texas right-wing culture, took to makeup like an artist to acrylics, defined and refined her goals and, when I looked up, that taciturn goth-girl had blossomed into this uncompromising young woman.

Three months ago, on graduation day, I felt like I'd won the Nobel Parenting Prize. Three months, but it was really a different lifetime altogether. The Saturday morning a week before graduation, I was sitting in that house in Texas at about this time—the morning after her Senior Prom. The mess aggravated me then and her absence frightened me a little. The phone rang.

I tripped over her backpack and almost fell on the coffee table. "Hey," I said.

"Hey," she said.

"Where are you?"

"Fort Worth, I think."

She'd worn a red gown and a tiara, her makeup was perfect and she and her friend Jessica had gone together. After the prom she was supposed to go to the high school gym for an "overnight lockdown."

"You think?"

She yawned. I could hear her stretching.

I said, "Where are you?"

"In a hotel."

"Whose room?"

"Some guy's."

Not exactly what a father wants to hear. "What are you doing?"

"Sleeping."

"With who?"

"Amy and Ryan."

"Where's Jessica?"

"On the floor."

"When are you coming home?"

"Later."

I heard someone laugh in the background

"I'll be home later. Don't worry, Daddy." She hung up.

Don't worry? I've been worrying for eighteen years. How do you turn that off? And how do you turn it off when she's in the hotel room of "some guy" with a bunch of teenagers. Okay. I worried. I was good at it.

The pile of videos on the coffee table didn't bother me too much, but the empty cereal bowl on the couch was starting to aggravate me. At least it was quiet. I turned on the stereo—whatever CDs she had in the carousel. I sang along to some mix of Pavement, the Pixies, Coldplay, and Soundgarden—yeah, I knew the names of some of the bands, but I didn't know which band did which song. There were six half-full glasses in her bedroom, one with quite a culture. I tripped over her guitar case and spilled red Kool-Aid down the stairs. I was lucky I didn't break my back. Damn kid.

The phone rang again. I avoided her backpack this time.

It was Heather. "I need directions."

"From Fort Worth?"

"Well, it turns out we're in Dallas."

"What did you do last night?"

"Nothin'."

"Where in Dallas?"

"We just passed Texas Stadium."

"Going north or south?"

"I don't know."

"Was it on your left or right?"

"Right."

"You're going the wrong way." I gave her directions, but didn't expect her home soon. When she figured out where they were, they'd find something to do.

A week later her aunt and grandma flew out and, the night before graduation, she invited us to a concert. Her friend's band was playing at a tiny theater. I leaned against the bar, my mom sat on a stool next to me, and Heather sat on a bench in the middle of the theater with her friends. I drank old scotch and watched those kids laugh together one last time. I'd known most of them since second grade and loved every one. Ryan, her boyfriend, the National Merit Scholar who got stoned every day, sat on her left but she was whispering to Shane, who sat on her right. He'd been such a geeky-looking little boy with that short black hair, glasses, pale skin, and scrawny body, but now he was the ultimate music-snob, his hair was bushy, he played every instrument and wore contacts. It was hard to conceive of him as cool. Her best friend, Jessica, saw me and danced over for a hug—dramatic and sweet, with bubbly smiles and an ability to at once care deeply what others think but go about her business anyway; Jessica practically lived with us.

I wondered if they knew that it was the last time they'd all be together.

The next day Heather walked across the stage at the Fort Worth Convention center and collected her diploma. And she was wearing a pink skirt. If you'd told me six years ago that Heather would wear a pink skirt to her high school graduation, I'd have laughed and defended her, "Nah, we wear black."

Once she'd graduated, there was no reason left to stay in Texas. After all those years, swimming in foreign seas, it was time for us to swim under the Golden Gate to a place where she couldn't even remember living but still thought of as home. We packed our stuff in a big yellow truck and drove away from that funny-looking wonderful house in that little valley. It felt strange to love that place but still want to leave.

We listened to Bill Clinton's autobiography on tape from Fort Worth to Phoenix. He'd say something that would strike a chord, she'd press pause and we'd argue for a few minutes, laugh for a few more, and resume listening to what Bill had to say. It was raining when we came down the hill out of Arizona and into California. I saw a rainbow in the rearview and pulled over. I got out of the car and looked back at the rainbow. Looked back at the life we'd left behind.

I leaned into the cab of the truck. Heather was digging through CDs. I said, "Check it out, we're somewhere over the rainbow." She stopped her CD search long enough to say, "*You are such a loser.*"

I thought she was asleep when we were crossing the Mojave Desert, which was a stupid assumption because I was singing Beatles songs at full volume. At least she waited until the next day to tell me how bad I sounded.

We got off the freeway north of San Francisco and drove to this tiny house in a cute little town in the wine country. The fog rolled over the hills in the afternoon, tendrils of cool moisture caressing the grape vines.

\*　\*　\*

"Check this out," I said on July 21, our second day in Petaluma. "It's late July and I'm wearing a sweatshirt." We counted the cars that still had Bush bumper stickers—both of them. We even caught ourselves looking for a corporate-chain restaurant. We couldn't have been farther from Texas if we'd been on one of Jupiter's moons.

Heather liked nothing more than driving to San Francisco. The first time she went alone she called me — she thought her car had been stolen. She'd parked right in front of Macy's at Union Square. I said, "There are no parking spaces in front of Macy's." She said that the curb wasn't painted red. I told her to find a cop and go get her car from wherever the Department of Parking and Traffic had towed it.

Crossing the Golden Gate Bridge was spiritual for us. We'd get all quiet and our eyes would well up. One time she said, "Life is too short not to live it in California." And I wondered if we should have moved home sooner, but the image of Heather and me living in our little valley in Texas came to mind and it felt like a gentle pat on the back.

Inside the tiny house we rented for three times what the mortgage payment had been in Texas, there were half-empty cups in Heather's room, cereal bowls on the coffee table, I couldn't find the TV remote, and damn, why did she have to leave her backpack there?

*     *     *

Summer ended and Heather packed her things. When I went to college I had two boxes, a suitcase, and a typewriter. For Heather, we had to borrow a pickup truck. We crossed the Golden Gate Bridge and pretended not to cry, drove over the mountains and up the hill to the Santa Cruz branch of the University of California. Nestled in a redwood forest on the slope of a mountain with a view of the ocean, it looked to me like Mount Olympus, safe and separated from the rest of the world, no better place to do that growing up that she couldn't do with me.

We carried her stuff to her room. I climbed up on the bunk bed while Heather set up her computer and put posters on the wall. My dorky kid had posters of senators—John Kerry, Bob Kerry, John McCain and Joe Biden—I'd had Aerosmith, Van Halen, and the Oakland Raiders on my dorm walls. Her roommate, Gwen, came in with her brother and both parents. None of them saw me up on the bunk bed. Heather introduced herself, shook hands with the parents, and tried to make a joke with her new roommate. Gwen's father asked about Ethernet connections in a whiny voice and her brother pointed out how the rooms were wired with an even whinier voice. Heather stole a glance at me and flashed a look that said, "Must I tolerate these losers?" Gwen's mother started making up her bed and fussed over little frames with little pictures as they came out of boxes. Gwen's father and brother set up her computer and couldn't get a connection.

Like the word of the god of technology from the top bunk, I said, "Just reboot the damn thing." Heather chuckled and climbed up on the bunk with me. She whispered, "Mr. McDorky and son." Gwen sat in her desk chair and watched her family unpack for her. Heather elbowed me and whispered, "You didn't help me ..." I whispered back, "Who was the guy who carried all your crap up that fuckin' hill?" Gwen and her family looked up at us for a second. I leaned over to and whispered in Heather's ear, "What did I do?" She whispered, a little too loud, "You said 'fuck,' bonehead."

Heather's other roommate walked in with a suitcase, a guitar, and a laptop. She was barefoot and wearing a long tie-die skirt. And she recognized Heather's Senate heroes. Gwenn and her family went out to dinner and I got to sit up on the bunk bed and watch Heather make friends with Sarah.

Sarah asked Heather about her major and Heather said, "Politics. What about you?"

"Art, I think, maybe music," Sarah said, then pointed up at Heather's posters. "How come you have John McCain?"

"He's lovely. He's like, got a soul and my dream-ticket is Joe Biden and John McCain. America would win."

"Really? But McCain is, like, well, isn't he a Republican?"

She said "Republican" the same way that you might expect a student at Texas Tech to say "Democrat."

I said, "And suddenly, after a lifetime as the left-wing radical, Heather is a moderate."

The "community assistant" came around and told the girls about a mandatory meeting for freshman. It started in fifteen minutes. I hugged Heather and walked down the stairs and along the path between redwood trees to the parking lot. I was excited and melancholy-happy. I'd never lived alone before, and seeing my little girl taking her first steps as an adult tasted sweet, but a little salty.

As I headed back over that mountain, I took my cell phone out of my pocket and called the dorm room. No answer. They were at the mandatory meeting, so I left a message to whatever roommate checked: "Heather likes to be called Boodle. She might deny it, but everyone always calls her that, so tell everyone you know to call her Boodle." I started calling her Boodle the day the nurse handed her to me. All wrapped up in that blanket she looked like a "Boodle." I don't know what a Boodle is either, but if you'd seen her you'd have called her a Boodle, too. She was the first baby I ever held and I took her in my arms the way a fullback takes a handoff when it's fourth and goal and the game's on the line. I tucked her up against my chest, one hand on her head, the other on her ass, my arms covering her and holding her tight. I held on tight for a long time, the whole way to the university. I protected her from hard-hitting safeties and cruel linebackers, from body-image problems and compulsive hair pulling, and I pushed her when she wanted to pause, and told her to rest when she was pushing too hard.

*     *     *

I sobbed the whole way over that mountain. I wanted her to grow up. I wanted her to fly away. But I never wanted those years we spent together to end. You know, parents think that they do all the raising and their children do all the growing, but that's not how it really is. Heather and I grew up together in our little valley and we left when it was time. She taught me just as much as I taught her and, so far, the greatest lesson that Heather has taught me is that paradise is fleeting. That it's harder to recognize paradise than it is to find it.

Here I am in this beautiful old house in this story-book, wine-country town somewhere over the rainbow, but the house is too fucking clean, I don't know what channel my favorite show is on—I don't even know what the name of the damn show is—and I never trip over anything when I answer the goddamn phone. EMTNSTR

# SHAKING OFF EMPTY

· *Wendy Cohen* ·

I WAS WELL PREPARED for having an empty nest; after all, I had a 'half-time nest"—joint custody—since my daughter was a year old. I went to school or worked full time, so I secretly cherished those Friday nights when Jennifer left for a week to be with her father and my house was silent. Granted, I was too tired to consider going out; my fantasies of freedom stretched to taking a hot bath, crawling into bed with a book, or going really wild and ordering Chinese food to pick up on my way home. It was a deliberate show of independence to eat it straight out of the carton, possibly over the kitchen sink.

My work required travel and long hours so my "week off'' was professionally my "week on." So, how bad could it be to not have to answer to anyone else's needs, cut my laundry loads in half, and not be concerned if I took too long in the shower and used up all the hot water?

It sucked.

All of a sudden I felt naked and exposed in my single status.

The structure of being Jennifer's mom kept me not only at soccer games and PTA meetings; it kept me from facing my loneliness. No amount of care packages and clever greeting cards could replace my need to nurture another human being. I now had to face the dismal state of my dating life and the support system I had not established for myself. All those years on the soccer sidelines I wasn't having in-depth conversations; we rarely got past who was bringing the cut-up oranges next week or what PG movie was currently playing. This was a paltry excuse for meaningful friendships. I quickly realized that over the years of mothering, I had abandoned my own friendships, and my nest wasn't the only thing that was empty. And despite all good intentions by the couples of the world, a single is a single and only to be included on special occasions.

I began a deliberate campaign to get busy. I upped the gym membership, upped my effort to go out with friends, even upped the state of my underwear in hopes of taking it off in someone else's company. I fell into a pattern of going out with several single women on Saturday nights. We were long past the "hooking up in bars" phase of life, so most often we were going to dinner and movies. One night I went out with a close friend and two women I didn't know well. We struggled through the remake of "Sabrina" (oh, for the romance of Audrey Hepburn and Humphrey Bogart!) and headed for dinner. During dinner, one of the women, Sandy, asked about my daughter. When I proudly told her that she was at UCLA, she looked at me and said, "Oh, you are going to end up just like me. Your daughter will stay in L.A. and you will be 50 and alone." I can't remember what I did yesterday, but those words stuck—and scared me to death.

A week later my management called me and asked if I would consider moving to New York. It had never been my dream or desire to be a New Yorker—I'm a California girl—but Sandy's words kept haunting me. There was no reason not to go and every reason to push myself out of the nest. I had no friends in New York, no clue of where you bought toilet paper or what a borough really meant. I said yes, and two months later my house was rented and I was calling Manhattan home.

I have never felt so alone in my life and when I wasn't lonely and scared, I had never felt so independent, so clear that I was making decisions just for me.

That summer, thick coffee milkshakes became my primary comfort food. I rewarded myself after I rode the subway—packed like sweltering sardines—or walked home on the steaming sidewalk. A cool shower, a collapse on the couch with a creamy chilled glass of calories and cholesterol, and I regained my sense of humanity on the nights when I couldn't face another moment of the frenetic city. When winter came and I found myself schlepping my groceries home from the store through sleet (it took me a while to discover the ease of grocery delivery), I traded in my icy salvation for cinnamon toast and hot cocoa. Thank goodness that by then I had discovered where the gym was.

Somewhere between the bad hair effects of humidity and the biting cold of winter, I also discovered that I could go to the movies, a play, or a museum by myself and really enjoy it. I learned to eat dinner alone in a restaurant without having to hide behind a book, and I learned that I was going to be okay, no matter what came next in my life. Yes, the nest was still empty—but the future was wide open and I had a whole new world to discover. And in New York, they delivered the Chinese food right to your door! EMTNSTR

# Part Four

# CH...CH...CHANGES IN THE FAMILY

# THE GOOD-BYE GIRL

## · Ronnie Caplane ·

I SEE THE HALF-FINISHED, small size, plastic bottle of Coca-Cola that my daughter left on the kitchen table 36 hours ago, and my throat tightens. Morgan probably thought she'd finish it. But now it's too late. By May, it will be too flat, too old, too disgusting to drink.

This morning she left to fly back to college and won't be back until May.

All day I feel strange, not quite sick but not really well either. I keep getting weird sensations like someone has just left the room, or like I've forgotten something.

I'm in the good-bye phase of parenting when your children become visitors rather than residents in your life. This year it's Morgan. Next year it will be Sammy too.

Even the dogs are depressed. My husband says dogs don't have extended consciousness; they don't remember today what happened yesterday. But he's wrong. When they saw Morgan walk out the door with her suitcase, they knew their affection, attention, and treat quotient was going south.

The pouring rain cheers me up. The synchronicity between my mood and the weather is comforting.

"Now you know what it means to have a hole in your heart," my friend Rita says. Her kids are younger than mine, but she knows.

* * *

Throughout the day my husband tracks Morgan's flight on the computer, a little bleep he flags as "Morgan's flight." He watches it ooch its way across the United States.

Periodically he sends me e-mails. "Morgan is leaving Utah and entering Wyoming."

It'll be four months before Morgan leaves Wyoming and enters Utah. Before that happens, I will have given the dogs four doses of heartworm pills, changed the Brita water filter twice, and replaced my electric toothbrush head once.

Of course, I'm thrilled that Morgan is adjusting so well and embarking on the rest of her life. All those life skills that we tried to instill are paying off. But did she have to adjust quite so well and quite so quickly? And I thought bittersweet only meant chocolate.

"Morgan just left Nebraska and is over the southeastern corner of South Dakota," Joe's e-mail says.

I zap one back.

"South Dakota? She's going to Boston. South Dakota isn't on the way. Are you sure you're watching Morgan's plane?"

This time Morgan was home for four-and-a-half weeks, 33 days. She slipped right back into the familiar routine of last year. Up and out early spending her days horseback riding. By 4:00 she'd be sitting on the kitchen counter watching television. And every day I reminded her to get her feet off the counter.

This was a long visit, almost long enough to forget she wasn't here to stay. But then something would remind me this was only temporary, like when she went out of town for a weekend. Saying good-bye felt bigger than what it was, like a rehearsal for what was coming. After that I woke up every morning and calculated how many days remained before she left.

I analyze the saying good-bye experience to figure out what's worse, my leaving Morgan at school or her leaving me at home. Leaving her at school is worse I decide. That's her world, one I'm not part of, concrete proof that her real life is separate from mine. She still calls this "home," but I know with time that will change too.

In the afternoon, I check the airline's web site and see that Morgan's plane has landed. I'm relieved she's safely on the ground but sad knowing that there are 2,704 air miles between us. In two hours, I'll call her at the dorm to make sure the last leg of her journey went well.

As I set the table for dinner, I'm painfully aware of taking out one less place mat and one less plate than I did yesterday. I know it won't take long to fall back into the routine of not having Morgan here. I have an extended consciousness and remember I adjusted before and will again and that there even are some good things about having one less child in the house.

But that's not how I feel today.

I pick up the bottle of Coke to throw it out, then change my mind and put it back on the table. Today is too soon. I'll take care of it tomorrow. EMTNSTR

# ONE BY ONE

## · *Risa Nye* ·

WHEN OUR THREE KIDS were younger, we spent part of our summer vacations at a beautiful mountain lake. During stolen moments alone while the kids played in the sand or splashed in the icy water, my husband and I tried to imagine what it would feel like when they got too big or too busy to spend lazy days with us on the beach. We calculated how old we would be when the baby graduated from high school: over fifty, but just barely. It was impossible to imagine then, but now here we are—back to the two of us in the blink of an eye.

The kids left home in the same order they arrived: my daughter first, followed by my two sons. Caitlin surprised us all with her strength and determination from the time she was a baby. Born with a congenital heart defect, she toughed it out for three months in intensive care. After that, we never doubted her ability to make her life what it was meant to be. She was a trailblazer: the first in our whole family to attend a liberal arts college on the East Coast.

The summer before she left, when she was jumping out of her

skin, I taught her how to knit. I wasn't sure what else I had left to teach her, so this seemed like a good thing to do. One day that summer, while still on vacation at the lake, my husband and I went out and shopped for things we thought she would need to take to college with her. We threw boxes of tissue and Q-tips and band-aids, soap and toothbrushes and shampoo into the cart, as if she wouldn't be able to find these things at college. It was silly, and we knew it, but it was something to do that seemed like helping. In August, when it came time for her to go, I drove my daughter and my husband to the airport. I swallowed hard and gave her a big hug—with a brave smile and a few tears, I watched her hitch her backpack over her shoulder and walk away.

During her freshman year, I inundated Caitlin with silly cards, an assortment of articles, newsy letters, and postcards of local landmarks like the San Francisco skyline and the Golden Gate Bridge. We sent her care packages and had weekly phone conversations—more when she was sick or just homesick, like when the endless first winter hit. This California girl of mine started saying things like, "We had snow today, but it didn't stick," as though I knew what that meant.

Without Caitlin around, I lost my best company for girl talk, knitting and shopping, and my husband lost his companion at baseball games. The boys carried on as if nothing had really changed. There was some jockeying for position at the dinner table and some groaning about doing the dishes more often, since their sister was out of the chore rotation. We got used to being four instead of five. Before long I geared up for teaching the next oldest how to drive.

I was delighted when Caitlin asked if I was coming to the first family weekend at her college, and promptly made arrangements to go. She looked almost the same, with her blue-green eyes and a halo of curls in a new shade of auburn; the California summer-sun streaks she'd left with were now disguised with henna. Her tiny dorm room was festooned with all the cards and pictures I'd sent. She introduced me to her friends, and we spent some precious time doing our favorite things: talking, knitting, and shopping. Now I could picture her in that room when she called, curled up on her extra-long twin with the lavender flannel sheets.

Three years later, we sent Myles, our older son, off to UCLA—a mere hour's airplane ride away and a manageable drive as well. He had no problem settling into his three-man dorm room. Although I worried about how he would do at such a large school, he found his niche among fellow actors, writers, and other creative types immediately. He called once a week and gave us the headlines about his life. It was easy to fly down to see him perform in musicals and plays, and I enjoyed walking through campus and meeting his friends.

On one visit, the summer before Myles's senior year, we spent the day getting him set up in his new off-campus apartment. I loved following him around as he filled shopping carts with linens, cooking utensils, and bookshelves. We set things up the way he wanted them, and by the time I left, the new curtains were hung, the coffee table was put together, and the dishes were stacked on the shelf. I knew what his home looked like and could picture him there when we talked.

When Myles left, my husband and I wondered how the family dynamic would survive the current shift from a 2:2 parent/child ratio to the double-teaming James, our youngest, would face for the next five years. We had not been an "only child" family for nineteen years, and were too naïve to appreciate it then. Now, we were down to one child, the youngest and quietest, who had flown under the radar for most of his life, often overshadowed by two lively, larger-than-life older siblings. What would happen when he was allowed room to grow? What would he make of a five-year sentence with the full attention of both his parents?

We worried that we might not have as much fun around the house with just the three of us, in the absence of our highly energized and entertaining older son. Our two blue-eyed boys had developed a rapid-fire form of verbal volley—parry and riposte—that often left observers breathless. They are evenly matched in these extraordinary exchanges of wit and humor, which amount to a fever-pitch improvisational war of words. No one makes me laugh the way they do.

But James rose to the occasion, participating in dinner table conversation with us about politics, history, movies, books, current events, and silly things as well. He took up fencing, worked on the school newspaper, got into acting, and played in the school jazz band. We went to more science fiction movies, art museums, and baseball games. He took up the mantle of his sister and accompanied his dad to many sporting events. Though we enjoyed it when the older kids came home, we found that we were quite happy to settle back into the routine we had established as a smaller, quieter family unit. Once again, and for the last time, I taught a kid to drive.

By the end of James's senior year, my husband and I were prepared to be back to two. Still, it was an emotional time gearing up for his departure, full of wistful looks back at the last five years. I was acutely aware each time I filled out a school form or went to a school play, it was for the last time. But James was clearly ready to take off, and we were happy that he had been accepted to the college of his choice, a small liberal arts college on the West Coast. There was a moment on that rainy moving-in day when we said good-bye, and it was not the teary Hallmark moment I had expected. It was an acknowledgment that an era had ended and a new one had begun for all of us.

The day we got back from dropping off our son, we looked at each other across the kitchen table, and decided it was time to take out the leaf. Without James as middleman, we couldn't pass each other the salt—my arms couldn't reach that far. Finally, it really hit home that we were, indeed, downsized. We dragged out the old copy of "Cooking for Two" we received as a wedding gift.

With all the kids gone, I threw myself into my work. I thought this would help me over the hump of having no kids around—which it did—but I missed seeing my son's face every day. I missed hearing him sing "The Star-Spangled Banner" in the shower. The hardest part was coming home to an empty house, especially when I got home late. I work at the high school my kids attended, so I had plenty of kids around me during the workday. For the first few weeks, I half expected James to pop into my office and bum a dollar as he used to do on occasion. That first winter, as the days got shorter, I felt a little mopey. I started writing more, often as soon as I got home.

With just the two of us here, our dinner hour has become more flexible, and sometimes we decide to go out spur of the moment. We are more spontaneous about a lot of things. We started getting the Sunday *New York Times* and going out for coffee, sometimes blowing half a weekend. Occasionally, we go to two movies in one day. We have discovered that after twenty-six years of having kids under our roof, we haven't lost sight of who we are as a couple.

And, we are having a lot of fun—even though we occasionally grumble about having to do all the household chores ourselves. Now, when there are crumbs on the counter, or we run out of milk or lose phone messages, we can blame only each other.

Today, our kids live in three different zip codes, scattered from Portland to Providence. We love to go see them, and we also love to have them come home to see us. We are seeing more of the world and trying to make a difference in our work. And sometimes, as we used to do on those long-ago summer afternoons, we still wonder what lies ahead for our grown-up children.

People told me when my kids were small that it all goes by in an instant. As a young mother, I never believed this because I was so distracted that each day seemed like pushing a rock up a mountain and the next day I got to do it all over again, with laundry.

Maybe it does go by quickly, and it can be harder than anyone thinks, but the way I see it, letting children grow up and go is part of the sequence of events that starts the first time they reach for that shiny object, just beyond their grasp. EMTNSTR

# Heavy-Hearted to Hopeful: The Healing Nature of Time

### · Joan Cehn ·

IT WAS LATE AFTERNOON when we returned home after leaving our daughter, and only child, 2,000 miles away to start her first year of college. I dreaded pushing open the front door and walking into the empty house. I knew what wasn't there. No soccer balls or cleats to trip over, no books on the floor, no running feet on the stairs, no voice shouting "Hi, Mom!" There was no longer a child residing here and the sadness of that was overwhelming.

I numbly walked into the kitchen and opened a cupboard to retrieve some tea. There lining the shelf were our daughter's cereal boxes, and I realized she would not be eating those for a very long time, if ever. I started to cry and my husband, who had been wandering around in his own personal daze, looked over at me. His eyes were wet, and blinking away the tears he exclaimed, "My life is over!" As he is an accomplished scientist, this struck me as hyperbole, yet I understood. All of our accomplishments seemed to fade away and our most valued job, the job of raising our daughter, seemed gone as well. We had centered our lives around her and now she had left to start hers.

I had not predicted the extent of my sadness. I assumed it would be fleeting and that I would readily see the positive aspects of her absence. I was puzzled as to why I was crying so much and troubled as to why I was not "moving on." It was embarrassing to discuss my feelings, because after all, going to college is wonderful and a sign of a parental job well done. And it seems like just plain whining. So I mostly kept it to myself. In time my husband seemed to adjust to life without her, yet I was still suffering. A new unencumbered life was not what I desired. I wanted the old one back—our small family living under the same roof. It had gone too fast and ended too soon. I was mourning the loss of our family, the one we had worked so hard to finally have.

*     *     *

It was in late October, about two months after her departure, that I stumbled upon an insight that explained, at least partially, the reason for my amplified sadness. We had adopted our daughter as an infant, and like many private adoptions, it had not gone smoothly. We had excitedly flown back east two days after she was born to meet her birth mother and to bring our new daughter home to start our long-awaited family. Events such as these do not always go as planned and after spending four days becoming acquainted with her birth mother and bonding with this most cherished baby, it became clear that we would be returning home without her, at least for the time being. Our birth mother needed more time. And so we returned home, just the two of us, not three.

Ah, that return home was devastating. We had expected to walk into the house with our baby in our arms; instead, we had left her 3,000 miles away, with the future uncertain. She felt lost to us, and for five weeks she was—until we were finally able to bring her home.

I eventually realized the parallels of the two empty homecomings. Upon returning home from the college drop off, the ghost of the eighteen-year-old memory had surrounded me and without conscious awareness I had became affected by its sadness and grief. The same questions surfaced:

"Will she be OK?"

"When will we see her again?"

"Will she forget us?"

And then came the descent of that long-forgotten feeling of emptiness in our lives. The similarities seemed to explain my exaggerated reaction to the feelings that many parents experience when leaving a child at school, yet our specific history had blown them out of proportion.

I slowly began to feel better. But I would be lying if I said I was now perfectly fine and redecorating her room. The memories of raising her are still so present, and I miss those earlier times. I find myself paying closer attention to young parents and their children and wondering if they appreciate the preciousness of this time in their lives. We had narrowly escaped being childless and deeply cherish being parents, and I wonder if they do too. I hope so.

I am now looking forward to our daughter's return for winter holiday. We had made a concerted effort to separate and let her be, and now it will be close to four months since I have seen her and my excitement is building. I am mentally planning activities for us to do together, and visualizing lazy evenings in front of the fireplace where she tells me all that has happened to her. I am eager to hear about her new friends and her new life. Yet, I am not that naïve. I have done my homework and know from my friends who have traveled this road that if I get a fraction of the time I am hoping for, I'll be lucky. So I am, on a more realistic level, preparing myself to accept whatever "parent time" is allotted during this holiday break. And after? Well, I am not yet comfortable with just e-mails and the occasional cryptic phone call. I struggle with visualizing the evolution of our relationship and the form it will take over the years. Yet for now, I realize that after the holidays, she will be off again on her journey and this is just a respite along the way. And for now, I am just the facilitator.

I have always believed that being a parent was the most important job I would have. My career took a backseat and I was grateful for that option. I was and still am my daughter's biggest cheerleader. I tried to raise her to know that she could accomplish anything and had endless choices. I know she is eager to someday make her mark in the world and to follow her dreams. I am proud of her and will encourage her all the way. And now it is probably time I start to take my own advice and make some marks of my own. EMTNSTR

## LAURA'S ROOM
### (From *No Place Like Home*)
· *Linda Weltner* ·

ALL WEEK, as the boxes have been piling up in the hall and shampoo bottles and sheets and sweaters and notebooks have been
disappearing into duffles, I have been impatiently muttering to
myself, "Just as soon as she leaves for college ..." as if I could
not tolerate the confusion of our older daughter's preparations
another second. As the contents of Laura's room slowly emptied
into the rest of the house, I have wished her away with a vengeance and longed for the peace and quiet that would soon take
the place of all her purposeful packing.

But now, without warning, I find my eyes filling with tears. It
suddenly seems very, very real. My first child is leaving home.

She's not going to Alcatraz, or even to a university halfway around the world. She will not be far away, or in pain, or
lonely, I hope, or even out of contact with us for long. She is
beginning the great adventure of her life, and it might seem no
more than an advanced version of the first day of kindergarten
if only she were not taking her favorite records, the puff she has
slept under since she was seven, and mementos that symbolize

all the experiences she has shared with us over the past eighteen years. I hear her moving in the next room, packing her curtains, "just in case" they fit her dorm windows, and in the pressure behind my eyes, I feel the message she has been broadcasting to us all.

*I am not planning on living here again.*

Into the attic go the stuffed animals, the diaries and letters, a thousand sheets of paper that describe a young life once entirely in our keeping.

"Why put them in the attic?" I ask. "Can't you leave them in your room?"

"I don't want to leave them hanging around," she explains. The place where they were once secure is no longer the place where they belong. There is nothing to argue about, no way I can win. "They are packing away their childhoods," comments a friend, and there is nothing we can do to stop them.

My friends' children have been leaving on a staggered schedule these last few weeks, each with his own style, her own symbolic gesture at parting. One girl leaves her room a mess, as if to reassure her mother that there is nothing special about this particular farewell. A boy unearths a journal he kept briefly in ninth grade and calls out, as his folks bid him good-bye at school, "You have my permission to read anything you find in my room." And one, pointing to a bathrobe left hanging in her closet, tries to deny the separation. "This way I can just grab a few things and come home weekends."

Some children go off without a backward glance, others dissolve in tears. A daughter teases, "You guys aren't going to forget me now, are you?" A son makes the last few months so difficult that all parties are initially relieved at the distance between home and school.

The mothers are not fooled for a moment. There is in every parting an amalgam of dread and anticipation, grief and relief that stems from years of mutual need. These mixed feelings co-exist with an inner urgency that cannot be denied. Fluttering at the edges of the uncurtained windows of my daughter's room and hiding in her empty drawers is the statement my child feels compelled to make as she approaches the departure that marks the end of her adolescence:

*You have to let me go.*

\*     \*     \*

It is worse than that. No matter how much we might want to "crush them small again," as the mother of a college freshman observed, we have to help them go.

One day after Laura's departure, the room next to my office is empty of life, an emptiness that hints of permanent loss. Don't remind me that Parents' Weekend is barely a month away, and our daughter's dorm no more than two hours down the highway. Don't tell me how fortunate she is or what a brave new future awaits her. Above all, don't tell me that today is the first day of the rest of my life.

I know as well as you do that every leave-taking represents a new beginning, but as I glance at the bare mattress in Laura's room, you will not convince me there is not a tiny death in every departure. EMTNSTR

PART FIVE

# INDISPENSABLE TO INCONSEQUENTIAL

# ONE SHOT

## · *Julie Renalds* ·

I AM SITTING across from Amy in an almost-empty restaurant in the village of Kinsale in County Cork, Ireland. After some lull in our conversation, Amy says to me quite suddenly and with some seriousness in her voice: "Are you going to be OK?" I knew exactly what she was asking—without her having to spell it out. If one were to spell it out, the rest of the question would have looked like this: "A-F-T-E-R  I  L-E-A-V-E  F-O-R C-O-L-L-E-G-E." It was weighing on her, as it certainly was on me.

"Of course I will," I lied. That's what I remember saying. After dinner, Amy and I walked back to our B & B; she was quiet—I suspected that she was thinking about her boyfriend back home, who had helped her pack and had tucked little love notes into her clothing and suitcase—notes that she would find during the trip, that I thought were making her even more homesick for him. I decided to give her some space, since I was feeling sad too—missing my husband Phil and that wonderful familiarity that home represents. I took the camera and walked straight up the hill behind the B & B, getting a little winded as I went, hoping that I could find something to make me feel a little happier so far from home. I walked for about 20 minutes when I came to this weathered white fence around some shrubbery. That's when I saw the farmhouse. My mood was instantly changed when I saw the sun setting behind the neat rows of crops, the old tractor, and the row of blackbirds resting on the fence that continued around the rear of the house. This is Ireland, I remember thinking. Beautiful beyond belief.

One click of the camera, disappointed I only had one shot left, I began to return when I thought to myself, "Just like being a parent—all you get is one shot." This trip—my last shot at really connecting with Amy before she headed to New York—felt disappointing to me. Amy was already weary of Kinsale and without a car, I guessed she felt like she had experienced all that "one of the prettiest small towns in Ireland" (according to the Eyewitness Travel folks) had to offer.

Of course, the trip took an upturn when we got back to Dublin and spent time with Amy's good friend Shannon and her family—but I couldn't shake the feeling that this was the "last something" before she left for school two-plus months later. I had been playing this sadistic little game with myself since the beginning of her senior year: Everything I did that involved Amy had the word "last" in it.

"This is the last time I'll ever go to an Open House."

"This is the last varsity volleyball game I'll ever see Amy play in."

"This is the last prom that Amy will go to."

I was in a prolonged mourning period that built to an emotional crescendo when Amy, her boyfriend, and I went to the

Oakland Airport to send her on her way to New York. In fact, it was at dinner that night when Amy asked if I would "be OK," that she told me she didn't want me to go to New York with her to move her into her dorm. She and her good friend/roommate-to-be were going to set themselves up on their own, thank you, without help from their parents. I was somewhat shocked but wanted to let her go with grace, on her terms. And so I did.

*   *   *

Was I OK when she left for her new life in New York? Of course not.

There were good days. There were lousy days when I couldn't get the hang of this "just the two of us" routine with Phil, in the home that used to be full of activity with Amy and her step-brother Jake. It was too quiet, she was too far away for "visits," and I was feeling untethered, lost at sea. One particularly bad day, my manager sent me home from work early (really early—like 10 a.m.), because I was an emotional wreck and not able to work with my usual attentiveness and care. During this same time, I also became better acquainted with Sauvignon Blanc as my alternative to chocolate (my comfort food of choice). It didn't happen overnight, but my well-marinated grief slowly lifted; testament to the fact that time does work its magic in healing. I also learned that healing is a process—a slow process at that; in my case, there were some milestones that marked the way.

I learned early on to stay away from the things that I knew would make me weepy: baby pictures, sitting in Amy's empty room, listening to CDs that I used to listen to with her. Sure, I indulged a little bit, but not enough to wallow in it.

When I was sad and my heart felt like it was stretched in every direction like Silly Putty on a newspaper cartoon, I would try to remember how Amy drove me crazy from time to time with monosyllabic answers or last minute requests for cash/a ride/laundry to be done. This helped—a little. Not a lot—I missed her; her presence, her laugh, and her wonderfully silly and accurate imitations of Stewart from MAD TV. I missed seeing her at the end of the hallway where she stood in the dark looking into my bedroom to see if she could speak with me by saying, "Mom?"

I found that savoring the good news and good conversations, however brief they were, helped to relieve the aching that I seemed to carry around with me like a too-heavy winter coat on a warm day. Hearing about a great grade or how the new roommates were fun to live with were the things that made it easier for me to not have her nearby. Family members would e-mail me or call to tell me the good news that they had received from Amy, all helping me to see the bigger picture: that she was happy following her dream, truly on her own in one of the most exciting and vibrant cities in the world.

Seeing Amy in her new college environment during Parents' Day that first October helped considerably. Tonic is the word that comes to mind when I remember seeing her for the first time in two months as she appeared in the dorm reception area. It helped to pull me out of my funk the way calls and e-mails were unable to do. To see her room, complete with her reminders of her old home (some satisfaction there for me that we weren't completely forgotten), was like swallowing that last dose of medicine that finally makes you feel like yourself again. Yes, it was very hard getting on the plane and leaving her behind this time, but it was also satisfying to see that she seemed happy, attentive to her studies, and not packing on the pounds as I did twenty-five years before when I was in college.

The most important lesson of all was that talking, sharing my pain with other parents really helped the most—eventually. This is where the first year was especially challenging. I was talking to others, but no one I knew seemed to understand the enormity of this transition. I saw a therapist for a few months until I stopped the visits because it wasn't what I was really searching for. What I desperately needed was to connect to other parents who felt somewhat the way I did. So I started a support/discussion group in my community. I placed a small ad in my local newspaper that announced "discussion group for parents whose children are leaving home." I had several responses within the first week—mothers who needed a forum as well, to talk, share, and listen about the challenging experience of letting go. I still remain involved in the meetings to this day, which not surprisingly have evolved to discussions of much more than the raw feelings of loss that many of us discussed during the first meeting. Now I view these times together as evenings with women that I enjoy, rather than an emotional lifeline that I once desperately needed.

So now, after experiencing Amy's partings after the holidays and at the end of her summer visits home, I can say that it has gotten easier to say goodbye. I am not ashamed to admit that while my two favorite words are still "AMY CELL" when flashed on my cell phone, I don't cry when she leaves anymore. I know that she is happy, that she is living her life in a way that is incredibly rich and independent, that I haven't held her back, and that she WILL be back, standing down the hallway again from time to time, giving me another shot at connecting with her again. EMTNSTR

# LEAVING HOME FOR COLLEGE

· *Penny Warner* ·

HIS BAGS WERE PACKED. His stuff was boxed. He was moving out.

After eighteen blissful years with us, making forts, filming movies, playing sports, and finishing last-minute homework, my son was moving into a Chico University dorm room with a view of its own.

On moving day, my son's bedroom was covered with overfilled boxes. He'd packed his TV, boom box, bedding, and *Star Wars* posters, leaving only a skeleton of his former bedroom. How would he manage without his dog Frosty, let alone his mother, I wondered? I thought about getting him a fish to keep him company on those lonely college nights. But he'd probably forget to feed it, like he did the last one.

As soon as he left to get more boxes, I sneaked into his room to check the status of packing, certain he would need my help. I found an old recipe for Rice Krispie Squares tucked in one suitcase and made a mental note to copy some other favorite snack recipes he might need when he gets hungry in the middle of the night. Better yet, I'd make the snacks and FedEx them to him.

Lying on one of the boxes was a clipboard with a list entitled, "Stuff I Will Need." After reading it over, it looked like he was packing for summer camp or some wonderful vacation spot instead of college up north: Guitar. Football. Frisbee. CDs. Books. Walkie-Talkies. Video Games. Phone Book. Camera. Snowboard. Dumbbells and Weights. Golf Clubs.

Half of that stuff he didn't even own. Apparently he was planning to "borrow" a few things from us.

Then I found another box full of very odd odds and ends. A flashlight. A tool kit. Some Band Aids. A set of markers. A couple of *Star Wars* figures. Did he really need all that stuff? I remembered when he could have survived overnighters with just a toothbrush.

I decided not to get all weepy and sentimental about his departure. I knew this day was coming. He'd changed a lot over the past few years and his lifestyle wasn't the same as ours anymore. He stayed out later, slept in longer, was rarely home for dinner, always with friends. He already had his own life. He was ready.

Living on his own at college would be good for him. In addition to academics, he'd learn real-life skills we could never teach him in the shelter of home. Like why he'd need to pay his phone bill on time. Like what happens when he partied too much and had to go to class the next day. Like what he'd do when he'd spent all his grocery allowance on guitar amps or skateboards and had to eat Top Ramen at every meal.

This is something he wanted to do. Even though we've given him free room and board, cooked for him, cleaned for him, bought him neat toys and cool clothes, offered him security and affection, he was ready to leave the nest.

It wasn't like I'd never see him again. I was sure he'd be back during semester breaks to do his laundry, eat a decent meal, or borrow some extra cash. Maybe he'd get tired of living with a bunch of guys who don't clean up after him, don't let him watch his favorite shows on TV, don't know he likes popovers for breakfast on Saturday, and his paper typed at midnight when it's due the next morning. Maybe when he ran out of clean socks, he'd realize he's made a big mistake going away to college.

But of course that wasn't going to happen. I had to accept the inevitable.

Three days after he left, I dialed the long-distance number and waited for the familiar voice to say, "'Lo?"

"Hi," I said too cheerily. "How was your third day of school?"

"Pretty much like the first and second day, Mom," my son said.

"Good. Good. How's the dorm? Meet any new people? How are your classes? Need any money?"

The answers were the same as the previous two phone calls: "Good. Yep. Fine. Nope."

I made sure that he was attending classes, eating the cafeteria food, and hadn't locked his key in the room. "OK then, well, have a good semester."

After I hung up the phone, I returned to his bedroom in search of anything he'd left behind that he might need. I could be on the campus in under three hours. Maybe stay overnight in an empty dorm room.

Inside I found his *Star Trek* trading cards, a videotape of *The Matrix*, and his old Pearl Jam CD. And this year's calendar featuring twins in swimsuits.

"Oh my god, he forgot all this stuff!" I said to my husband in a panic. "We have to take these things to him. Let's go!"

"Relax," my husband said. "He's fine."

He was right. I missed my son, but he was doing fine—and I would be fine, too. Someday. In the meantime, I started a scrapbook for him, filled with leftover memorabilia from his room, like graduation invitations and college application forms. I made a "Welcome Home, Son!" banner for his return at the end of the semester. And I mailed him some Chocolate Crinkle Cookies. His favorite.

As for me, I've accepted the fact that I won't be making popovers for a while, or washing blood from football uniforms, or digging for retainers in the trash bin at McDonalds. I guess it will be nice to still find some food left in the refrigerator, walk through the house without stepping on an athletic supporter, and listen to good music at a reasonable volume.

But if he needs me, I can be there in under three hours. With still-warm cookies. EHINSTR

# Time Makes You Bolder/ Children Get Older

· *Kate Wheatman* ·

I HAVE HEARD THE PHRASE "heart-wrenching" many times, but it wasn't until I dropped my daughter off at college for the first time that I learned that this term describes an actual physical sensation. As my husband and I pulled out of the campus parking lot, I was surprised to experience an intense ache in my chest which felt like something being ripped from my body. This may sound overly dramatic, but I guess my body was symbolically acting out the emotional separation from my first-born child.

It wasn't like I hadn't prepared for this moment. Actually, in many ways I had been getting ready for this good-bye for the past eighteen years. Laura is the older of my two daughters and was starting her freshman year at college in Oregon. We had both survived all the transitions of the past eighteen years including the stressful multiyear buildup to college—worrying about whether grades, scores, and activities were competitive enough; spending hours on the web researching colleges; and touring schools in our home state of California and the Pacific Northwest. We had made it! Laura was accepted at her first choice college. She was ready to start the next phase of her life, but was I?

As we headed south on the highway toward our Bay Area home, I wasn't really worried about Laura. From the moment we visited this college in the spring of her junior year of high school, Laura fell in love with the school. She said she felt "at home" there. Her Dad and I shared her sentiments. We could see her fitting in and being happy. We got the sense that people looked out for each other at this small liberal arts college and that our precious daughter wouldn't be just a number there.

Laura was never one to beg to go away to camp or to take one of those impressive overseas summer adventures that so many of her classmates had experienced. Even though she had never been away from home on her own for more than a five-night stretch, I could see that she was now ready to take this next step. As we passed the late summer hills of Oregon, I remembered when Laura had started kindergarten thirteen years earlier. Many of the other children were crying and frantically clinging to their mothers. As I felt tears building behind my eyes, Laura marched up to the front door with a wide smile, her carefully-braided pig tails swinging—and without a backward look began her educational career. I guess we all reach certain points in our lives when our doubts and fears fade and we just know it is time to move on. Beginning kindergarten and starting college were such times for my daughter, but on this August afternoon I questioned whether I was ready to let her go.

During the ten-hour drive home, I silently sobbed for much of the trip. What would my days be like without my exuberant daughter in the house? With my much quieter husband and other daughter and I at home, who would liven up the place? Would Laura and I stay close? Would she get so caught up in moving on with her new life that she would leave us behind?

We finally made it home and life with Laura away began. I was glad to see Rebecca, our younger daughter who was just starting high school. I was eager to get busy at work and to see my friends. But for the first two weeks I felt like someone had died, as melodramatic as that may sound. I walked around with an empty feeling and in private moments would steal away for a few tears. I kept busy but my heart wasn't really in it. Then after two weeks, the sorrow just faded. Life was going on for me just like it was for Laura. New patterns and routines emerged. Of course, I still missed her but the pain was gone, replaced by a great interest to hear about her college experiences and a desire to find new ways to make my own life meaningful to me. I was struck by the adaptability that we humans share. I had thought that I would feel miserable for months, but that wasn't the reality. I was amazed and pleased to experience the truism that life goes on and to realize that even at my advanced age I could optimistically enter a new phase.

I have found ways to adjust to life without my daughter at home. Whenever I miss her, I remind myself that she is where she needs to be and happy to be there. Fortunately, she realized right away that she did in fact make a good college choice. She also had the good fortune to be assigned a great freshman roommate who has become her best friend, and to enjoy her first semester courses and professors. I know if she had started out being miserable at school for whatever reason, I might not have had such an easy adjustment.

Right from the beginning I tried to work out ways to communicate with Laura without being overly intrusive. I didn't want to be one of those annoying mothers who is always calling to "check in." Yet I was so curious to hear about her adventures. We agreed that Laura would call home once a week on Sunday mornings at whatever hour she arose. I have to admit that I still look forward to that call each week and during the week I actually jot down notes so I won't forget all I want to ask her. I vowed to myself that I wouldn't call her unless it was urgent. I'm proud to say I have kept that promise. Of course, we told Laura that she is always welcome to call us any time if she needs to. There have been some traumatic times during her years at college—a breakup with her boyfriend, a junior year roommate from hell who was filling in for Laura's best friend who spent the year abroad, a professor for a General Education science course who thought that all students in my daughter's major (Theater) were incapable of understanding his curriculum and were destined to fail the course—when she has called us fairly frequently. Most of the time, though, she is able to handle her life just fine on her own and a weekly call home is all she needs.

I am an enthusiastic e-mail and AOL Instant Messenger (IM) user. These technological tools have enabled me to send brief notes or get a sense of what Laura is up to without feeling like I am bothering her or intruding on her privacy. I get a kick out of checking Laura's clever IM away messages which give me a clue (sometimes cryptic) as to what she is doing at that moment.

We manage to see Laura on average about every six weeks with Parents' Weekend, Thanksgiving and winter and spring breaks. That tides me over. I do have to admit that as the visit approaches, it begins to feel like Christmas to me. That first sight of my daughter is a joy. So far she has come home for most of the summers, but I know those extended visits won't last much longer.

I have built my daily routines without Laura and have tried to expand my own horizons. I do my best as a mother to my younger daughter. Rebecca is an independent girl whose first priority is her active social life. Between friends and school—and with a new driver's license and car to drive—she is off leading her life much of the time. She probably felt ready to go away to college at age 14. I don't feel she needs me too much on a daily basis but then something occurs where I see that she is still a kid in many ways and needs me for support and understanding. I put my energy into work and a new consulting practice. For the first time since having children, I traveled with women friends, taking trips to Italy and up the California coast. I have found time for long walks, yoga, and community service. My husband and I can just pop out on the spur of the moment to catch a movie or eat out. These are the compensations.

*   *   *

Now Laura has been at college for almost three years. She has grown more independent and mature while retaining her spark and exuberance. Although she and I have always been close, there is less friction between us now. I am no longer in a position to tell her what to do but am there if she wants advice. We can have more fun together because I think she feels that I am not judging or pushing her.

In a little over a year, Laura will graduate from college and plans to settle in Oregon. Rebecca will leave home for college somewhere yet to be determined. Another transition awaits me. I know it will be hard for me in many ways yet my experience with Laura going away to college has taught me that I can adjust and re-create my own life just as the younger generation is re-creating theirs. EMTNSTR

# Indispensable
# to Inconsequential

### · Joan Passman ·

THERE MUST BE SOME MISTAKE. For eighteen years I was the center of the universe in my family. I was the one who filled empty dressers with clean clothes, filled empty stomachs with healthy food, filled minds with possibilities, and filled souls with love as big as the Kansas sky. My husband and I took our youngest to college, and then drove home to the silence. My children, my reason-to-be, no longer needed their closets, stomachs, and minds filled by me. Being indispensable ended in one moment as Hilary and Zach moved into their future and left me with mine.

I thought about the many times I asked them to pick up their clothes, turn down the radio, close the door, get off the phone, do their homework, put things back where they were found, go to bed, turn the light off, set the table, eat the vegetables, walk the dog. All the negatives I said throughout the years; don't eat with your mouth full, don't talk back, don't blame others for your actions, don't roll your eyes at me, don't run the shower for twenty minutes, don't do this, don't do that. Now all the towels are hung neatly on the rack, the dishes are put in the dishwasher, the kitchen stays clean. No one eats the food that was meant for dinner. No one keeps the telephone busy for hours. Now that they are gone, all those instructions seem so tedious, and I would like to take back the words I spoke in anger.

I certainly knew this day would come. Part of my job as a parent was to help my children become independent, contributing citizens. The goal was to send them into adulthood with as much self-confidence and knowledge as I could stuff into them while they were in my care. As a plus to this launching, I would not have to listen to their music at top volume, listen to the moaning when they had to be up early for school, listen to the incessant ringing of the telephone, and listen to the complaints of unfairness when they were asked to cut the grass or clean the kitchen. I thought I was prepared for this stage of my life.

As I sat on the couch, staring at the wall, wondering how I would define myself if not as Mom, the word inconsequential came to mind. Oh no, that's pathetic! Surely there is still a Self inside the Mom. And so began the process of redefining myself as a separate and individual woman with a lot of time on her hands.

The one thing that has always felt good for my sagging ego has been volunteer work. Meals on Wheels offered a chance to continue cooking for more than two, to continue feeling needed, and to continue helping people become more independent. Eventually, I became the one in charge as president of the board. I love to read, so I began working part-time at a bookstore. I like feeling part of a community, so I began working part-time at the Chamber of Commerce, bringing new members into the organization. I became a member of the Democratic Town Committee, again helping me feel connected to my community and part of what I thought of as a good cause. The old adage about doing what you like to do and finding somewhere to plug into that work was good advice for me. These endeavors got me outside of myself and into the world of adults who had the same interests as I had. I was nurturing myself for the first time in more than twenty years.

That all happened twelve years ago, although the feeling of those days is boldly imprinted in my memory. During the college years, the children were home for weekends and holidays, in and out with friends and activities, but I realized they were just passing through, just visiting. Their trips home became less frequent as they immersed themselves in their own lives. Finally, it was done. They moved to other cities after graduation, got jobs, got married, bought homes, and had children.

As this process evolved, I let go of their childhood and began to enjoy them as adults. It amazed me that they had become so responsible. They appreciated me as a person and not just as their mother. They asked for advice, for recipes, for memories, for the continued affection between us as a family. We began fitting into each other's lives as equals. I realized that they were accomplished in ways that I wasn't. I could ask for their educated opinions and make use of their knowledge. This was going to be all right after all. No, it was better than all right. There was to be new energy in our family. The children were gone and the adults in their places were wonderful. Friendship was added to our love for each other. The old days retreated and our newly forged relationship began. They were back. EHTNSTR

# Off to College and On to the Roller Coaster

*· Eve Young Visconte ·*

I WAS NEARLY 40 when our first and only child, Nathan, was born. I was exhausted and just wanted to sleep, but suddenly I didn't have a choice of when to sleep. He would be my son, presumably for the rest of my life. I'd never been a parent, and it scared me to death. I didn't want to screw up this perfect child.

Somehow we muddled through as parents, and before we knew it, he was a senior in high school, sending out a "gazillion" college applications and stressing out over his SAT scores. We were all relieved when the last application was finished, and we just had to sit back and await the answers to his future: where he would go to college. The summer seemed long, and yet it flew by, and pretty soon, we were getting him ready to go off to UC Berkeley.

In a fog, we helped him pack. It was a very chaotic and stressful process. The physical part of the move was madcap, but over very quickly. We went out to lunch together, and it didn't really seem real. We waited to meet his roommate, and to have an early dinner with them at the dining room. It still seemed surreal.

We finished dinner quickly, kissed Nathan good-bye, and left in silence.

Why wasn't I crying? When we walked in the door, immediately the place felt empty. I took one look at the place, turned to my husband, and said, "Let's get the hell out of here." Doing what we do naturally to relieve stress, we picked up the *San Francisco Chronicle* and looked for a movie to see—anything, anything to put off the inevitable. The era of the empty nest had just begun.

The next day I had to fight off the urge to phone Nathan. I e-mailed him instead. My husband, Ron, said that I shouldn't have. I couldn't help myself, and I stressed out when I didn't get any answer either by phone or e-mail. I did what I do naturally—I started to worry. Was he OK? Was he mad at me / us? How was it going to be at Berkeley? Had he made the right decision? Ron kept reassuring me and warning me that I had to give him his space. "It's a guy thing," he told me.

I spent the next two months or so bursting into tears without any provocation. My husband was somewhat bewildered because, although he missed Nathan, he was starting to enjoy the quiet and the gift of time. He didn't know how to comfort me. Mistakenly, I confessed to my sister-in-law that I was bursting into tears all the time. Wrong person. Her reply was, "You've got to let him go." What the hell does she know about it? She doesn't have kids. Just shut up and let me grieve, please!

After about a week, we started receiving e-mails from Nathan, and he began to pour his heart out to us. He was homesick (he didn't say it in so many words, but it was clear). He still loved us and still needed us. All was not lost. He even called a couple of times during the year to ask us to come over for dinner with him.

He came home from time to time, and sometimes it almost felt like he was "back," but not quite. It was different, and thus began the next part of the empty nest syndrome—the roller coaster.

A friend told me about a wonderful book about the transition to college called *Letting Go.* It was the most comfort I had received since Nathan went away to school. The book outlined everything that we'd been through up until and including freshman year—to a "tee." Nathan was normal! Perhaps we'll all make it through. The description of the beginning of his experience was so accurate that I felt comfortable in reading about what's coming up as a kind of crystal ball for his future.

Ron, having had more low-key, "guy-like" reactions to Nathan's leaving, was beginning to feel like we were losing the emotional connection with him. This began over the summer and as part of his sophomore year. I told Ron, "Read the book. It's all in there." And it is. Freshman year is traumatic, and they still aren't completely separated from home. That separation comes during the sophomore year. Right on schedule—he seems more distant. We see him for short superficial visits. He doesn't communicate with us much—he's got a girlfriend for that. He's not sure what he wants to study, his motivation is down: he's in sophomore "slump."

How are we doing as empty nesters? We're now used to him being away most of the time. When I think about that, I get sad. We moved over the summer and so his room is new and in disarray, which makes it feel like he's not living with us anymore (even though we have designated a room for him and view him as an intermittent resident). His life is really fast-paced and fly-by-the-seat-of-your-pants right now, which drives us crazy. Let's face it, we're middle-aged, and the life of a nineteen-year-old is very different—loud, spontaneous, unpredictable, and up and down, emotionally as well as physically. The roller coaster the book talks about is right in our living room when he's here. He goes out with friends at 11 p.m., comes in at all hours of the night, and sleeps until noon or beyond. Totally topsy-turvy.

In contrast, the life of an empty nester is calm and slow-paced. We can do whatever we want, when we want to—or do nothing at all, which we often opt to do. After eighteen-plus years of putting his needs first, I confess, it feels great. But then I feel empty, and I sometimes want to cry. I'll read something about a college student in distress, or a car accident, and I worry about him. Could he be one of the "distressed" college students discussed in the book?

I keep telling myself, one day at a time, one crisis at a time; the roller coaster will eventually stop. We'll get through this and come out on the other side with a wonderful, bright, kind, educated son, who will again want to spend quality time with us—as a fully grown, separated adult. Thinking ahead to the time when the roller coaster stops, and we are reconnected with our beloved son, I smile. I've lost my little boy, sort of, but I've gained a grown son. Keeping my fingers crossed that this transition to his adulthood goes as planned, I look forward to seeing the fruits of our parenting, and trust that we have done a good enough job that we will have a long and happy relationship with an emotionally well-balanced productive son. I'm not religious, but this is my prayer: May it be so! EMTNSTR

PART SIX

# BITTERSWEET PARTINGS

# When a Son Heads off to College, the Parents too Begin a Journey

### · *C.W. Nevius* ·

WE FINALLY PUT a *New Yorker* cartoon up on the door to my son's room.

"I've made a list of all the things you'll need to take before you leave," it says. "So you can freak out in some kind of order."

We keep saying we are not losing a son—we are gaining a guest bedroom. But right now, I don't really want a guest bedroom.

It is happening all over the country, of course. First-year college students are packing up, hugging family members, and are walking, clear-eyed and resolute toward a future on their own. Meanwhile, the parents are fluttering around the suitcases, telling long-winded stories about the first day of kindergarten, and calling out questions that even they know are pointless and irrelevant.

"Did you pack nail clippers?"

We've certainly run this "last" thing into the ground. The last summer at home, the dinner out as a family, the last chance to remind him four times to bring in the trash cans.

"Well," I said, cluelessly last week, "I guess this is the last Friday before you go."

And a great silence fell over the land.

"Way to lighten the mood, Dad," his sister said.

Well, frankly, it is a little hard to keep up with the mood.

We have alternated between giddy excitement at starting this epic life change and moony memories that have us all changing the subject. It's the timing that is hard to get right. One minute we come across an old photo of him, a six-year-old on roller blades, grinning at the camera, and we feel an empty sadness. But that's at the exact moment that he's rushing out the door, yelling over his shoulder that he's on his way to coffee with his college-bound pals.

And then, when we think we've caught the tone and are kidding around, it turns out that he's been brooding over whether he has the right wastebasket for his dorm room. (He does. It is understated, yet functional. Well worth the two-hour trip to pick it out.)

What we've decided is that most of the important crossroads in life pop up unexpectedly. You meet your life partner at a party or a coffee shop. You happen to change jobs or careers on a fluke. An illness strikes you, or someone you love, without a hint of warning.

But there are only a few times when you know about a life-changing moment well in advance and can plan for it. There's marriage, the birth of a child, and leaving home. Today, tomorrow, and for months after this, the door will shut on a departure of a child from a home. Although it is a natural order of things, it is also wistful.

(You don't want to overdo the wistful, of course. Once, when I wrote a column about kids leaving home, a reader wrote back to say, "Yes, it is sad when they leave. But what is really sad is when they move back in.")

So sure, we're glad that they are so ready to strike out on their own. There are families who are proud to see their sons and daughters march away in uniform, ready to face what could easily be life-or-death experiences. Going away to school, or to an apartment in the city, pales compared with that, but it is still part of the grand scheme of letting go—as gracefully as possible.

We can all use some work on that. Part of the problem is knowing what is going to trigger the nostalgia turbo-drive.

Our family has a long and consistent history of terrible photography. Honestly, a lot of times it is hard to tell what we were even shooting. Needless to say, digital cameras have been a huge help. We can now take hundreds of murky, poorly composed photos at a time.

We have one of my son and me at a body of water. Might be a lake or the ocean. (We also have problems labeling our blurry photos.) But what it looks like is that it is one of the first times he's learned how to skip rocks. It shows my son, a little more than waist high, winding up to fire a rock into the waves while I stand next to him, clearly deeply interested.

At least that's what I say it is. To be honest, the figures are so badly backlit that you'd have to be a member of our family to recognize us. You can hardly make out our faces and we appear to be wearing clothes made from sewn shadows.

But I know who it is. And I don't know if it was a lake or the ocean, but I remember that moment. I look at that picture and I can only think of one thing.

Now who am I going to turn to when I need some advice? [EMTNSTR]

# THE OTHER SIDE OF THE SONG

· *Bill Coy* ·

LIKE MANY BUSINESS TRAVELERS, I try to numb/entertain myself
with the serendipity of "shuffle" on my iPod. This black and sil-
ver metallic box holds my entire music collection, short stories,
interviews, poetry, and podcasts. My tidy traveling companion
has more memory than I do, but at least mine is tied to people,
events, and emotions.

I was about two and a half hours into a flight from San Francisco to Washington, DC, when Tom Rush's "Child's Song"
slipped from the ear buds. It took me immediately back to 1973.
More emotion than memory overcomes me; a 51-year-old man
instantly becomes 18 again. The sense, the song, the memories
put me in that small house in Phoenix, Arizona, and tears begin
to roll down my cheeks.

"Child's Song" is sung in the voice of a young man leaving
home and saying good-bye to his mother, his father, and his
little sister. His perfect eighteen-year-old wisdom tells his father
that anger is not the answer, tells his mother to love the right
one, and tells his sister that her time for leaving will come soon

enough. The lyrics convey bitterness and redemption, hope, and forgiveness.

As a senior in high school, I sat in my room and listened to that song over and over again. I held a longing, more than anything, to get out of there, to escape actually. Most kids want to leave home; I needed to flee. My father had retired from the military five years earlier, and I had no memory of him being sober from 1968 to 1973. High school was a time of fists through walls, black eyes, and excuses. He was a man who raised drinking, indolence, disengagement, and anger to an art form, and everyone in our family suffered for it.

What terrifies us men more than anything is incompetence. We will flee from events and people that bring light to the dark places inside of us that we would prefer not see. For my part, I believe the reason we as men don't embrace fatherhood like women embrace motherhood is that it touches our longing for something we really missed and we don't know if we can provide this missing experience to our own sons. Nothing will drive a man to the precipice faster than not knowing how to do or be something. My own deepest fear is that, having no model, or truthfully a poor model, I would be a really lousy father. The song touched me because it was asking me the hard questions, "Did I do a better job than my father? Have I given my son more, loved him more, and been better to him than my own father had been to me?"

When David left for college, it struck me that I was now on the other side of the song. But it is a different song. David did not flee; he left like he had to leave. I took him to UC Santa Cruz and helped moved him into his dorm room. It was really a joyful day. Every box walked up every stairway was a step for the two of us. We were both starting new chapters, with me knowing that I had done the best job that I could, and him being happy—not because he was leaving someplace, but because he was moving towards something. He was not running away, he was running towards.

Carl Jung once said that whatever is in the unlived life of the parent becomes the burden of the child to bear. When my own father died I was a senior in college. It was the first time I can remember feeling empathy for him. He ran away from home when he was 16, lied about his age, and joined the army, where he spent most of his life. In many ways I never knew him, never learned from him what he could have taught me. So what were the lessons I had to teach my son as he left on this new chapter of his life? How could I teach something that I did not know? Have I lost my chance to be a good father?

When I look into my son's eyes, I see more gratitude in him than I ever saw in the mirror. Most of the time I feel unworthy of him—falling short of the type of father he deserves. At each transition point in his own life, kindergarten to grade school to high school, I promised myself that I would be a better father, become more engaged, present to him. I could see that he wanted the same thing I did. We are both sons, and I feared handing him the disappointment I was given.

We all have to leave home and leave something behind. My hope is that I have taught David how to pack for his journey. I want him to bring a sense of self, compassion for others, strength, and thoughtfulness. I see these qualities in him but feel that I had little to do with them.

My son told me that I have taught him well. He has shown me such gratitude, mixed with longing. Is it too late for me to continue to try and be a better father? Maybe not.

*    *    *

I snap back to the present. I have to be comforted, knowing that quite possibly I did the best I could; maybe even my father did the best that he could. Something, that until recently, was not even possible to contemplate. The lyrics could be the same, but I hope it is a different song that David would sing. **EMTNSTR**

# A Bittersweet Parting, an Empty Nest

### · Al Martinez ·

AND SO SEPTEMBER COMES, an intermingling of mist on the ocean and heat in the Valley, teasing with its hint of a new season but clinging to the old.

Also arriving, this election year, is an increase in the clanging and banging of presidential campaigning, with its assertions, accusations, recriminations, and denials.

Big lies triumph over feeble explanations, and cynical manipulations twist truth into distorted forms. The spin-doctors are back, leading us into a looking-glass world where things are never what they seem.

Global priorities change even as sunlight burns through the September mists, bringing tomorrows of uncertain peril, like the movement of ghouls at the edge of the forest. We sense, in the scariest of ways, that something's out there, something's coming.

I admit to no small amount of bewilderment as news of major occurrences explodes like mortar shells around me. Iraq!

France! Sudan! Israel! Shrapnel sprays our serenity and wounds our minds. Confusion always follows loud explosions.

And yet, the ordinary often prevails in the midst of chaos. We hide in small places of convenience to protect us, if only for a moment, from the flying shells. We turn to smaller problems and less cataclysmic changes. For instance, a new silence permeates our house. Teengirl has gone away.

She left one cool and sweet-smelling morning, before the sun had done its work, to catch a plane going east, lugging her teddy bear and her talent to a dorm at the School of the Art Institute of Chicago. A little excited, a little nervous, a little afraid.

I realize that you may not perceive this as an event of cosmic proportions. Not at all in the same league as political quests for power or military steel rolling over the bones and soft tissues of human bodies. And, of course, it isn't.

But still ...

Our Teengirl, a granddaughter, has lived with us for a year, seeking the time and distance that heals family rifts, and has filled our home with her presence. Artistically gifted and fiercely independent, she has pouted, laughed, cried, shouted, hugged, and floated through our lives and left us with the stillness of a passing storm.

Frantic, last-minute packing characterized her final night before leaving for Chicago, necessities delayed until the clock ticked toward midnight, her dalliance rooted, at least partially, in a longing not to change but to remain a child, with a child's toys and a child's freedom.

Winnie the Pooh never grew up, and Peter Pan flies forever through the skies of Never Never Land, but these are the characters of make-believe, shielded from the real world by the magic of imagination. In reality, no amount of longing can turn the years backward. Time is relentless in its forward journey.

Our Teengirl sought her place in Chicago with the persistence of an Olympic athlete, regardless of what inner feelings for home and safety she might have possessed. Her artworks, a portfolio of sketches and watercolors, were her impressive credentials into a new world.

But now, this dawning September, it isn't art, it's emptiness that commands attention, leaving us a little at a loss to fill the place where Teengirl stood. I walk into her room. Shoes are thrown into a corner, clothes are scattered like debris in the wake of a storm, dresser drawers are left open. Evidence abounds of her having been there. Even her turtle, left in our care, pokes through the surface of his water and peers through the glass of his tank to search for her.

Seeing Teengirl through her final year of high school to the freedom of her eighteenth birthday and to her first steps toward the future has been an experience we had never anticipated when we waved good-bye to our own children years ago. But in a family of high emotions and unbending attitudes, events occurred that brought our granddaughter into our home. We are, after all, the sum of our genetic combinations, passing on glints of steel and heads tossed in defiance.

We were given a second chance, Cinelli and I, to help raise a teenage girl, and I'm not sure we did any better, or any worse, a job than we did with our own two. No book exists to guide one through the shifting attitudes of adolescence or through moods that snap in and out of focus like rapidly moving objects viewed through a lens. Teengirl's parents did the best they could and we did the best we could, and now to her falls the responsibility of doing the best she can.

Meanwhile, at this moment, the war goes on in Iraq, hatreds bristle along the West Bank, France struggles with a life-or-death hostage dilemma, and the quest of two powerful men for the presidency of a land we occupy at its time of darkness demands that we make a choice for incumbency or revitalization.

And September passes with mist and sunlight through a new emptiness in our lives. EHTNSTR

# Her Independent Streak Runs at the Speed of Life

### · Al Martinez ·

TEENGIRL IS BACK in art school. She left our house like a vanishing storm, taking with her the noise and flurry that often accompany meteorological disturbances.

Her room had a faint post-apocalyptical look to it as she rushed out the door and headed for Chicago, seeking a new world of independence far away from the burdening influences of adults.

We've hardly heard from her since.

This is her second year at the Art Institute of Chicago and, at 19, her declaration of independence. It is the nature of young adults to be simultaneously dependent and independent as they search for the core of who they are, and it is not for me, or anyone else, to say what is right or wrong in the manner they pursue themselves.

*     *     *

Teengirl came to our house after a breakup with her parents in the heat of a quest to define herself. We guided her through her senior year and into college and now I sense she is shucking off the last little-girl memories that connect her to us.

I write of this today with mixed emotions of sadness and understanding. I joke that she is hidden in a witness-protection program, existing in a world devoid of the authority that was parental in nature.

She has begun a new life, Chapter 1 in her future, past those years that were simply prelude to the plot of life's book. We're all writing our own narratives each day of our lives, but it requires a certain esprit to make them interesting. One must dare and deviate in order to strengthen the plot. Surprise is the essence of an interesting life.

I know all that. I broke away from a dismal existence when I was about 17, went off to college, married, and joined the Marine Corps and to hell with what anyone thought about it. I didn't ask for advice from parents or friends. I just did it.

Teengirl's quest embodies my own declaration of individuality. I disliked what I had at home and swore it would never be repeated in my adult life, and it never has been. No child of ours was ever beaten or denied the goals they chose to pursue. I understood confinement of the soul and would not be anyone's jailer.

Teengirl was born with an amazing talent to paint, rooted in the genes of her parents and her grandparents, all possessed of the instincts to write or to draw. She began about age six creating cartoon characters with startling facility and has never stopped developing a skill to paint, sketch, and create in many artistic forms. Art school is demanding that she study them all.

But with that inner fire comes bursts of outer heat, explosions of temperament that can leave one treading backward away from the flames that the burst produces, not unlike the sudden eruption of a long-dormant volcano. Combine that emotional transience with a determined quest for independence and one has a volatility that cannot be easily damped.

As grandparents, we exist in a strange, almost surreal world. While lacking parental authority, we somehow come to represent it by establishing the rules that govern the parameters of a normal household. But rebellion brooks no status quo, and Teengirl found herself resenting what we had seemed to become.

She has defined our world as a separate reality from the one she occupies, and I don't argue with that. We all move about in parallel planes, which is how we manage to survive and, hopefully, achieve as individuals among the noisy crowds. Our rebellions are signified by clenched fists thrust high above the pack.

Teengirl's is moving upward.

But while trying to understand the psyche that propels a young woman toward a book of her own life, one misses the little girl of dependency that emerges in photographs and in the indelible memories of her years in her own home and in ours. One longs for the sweetness before the storm, as she began the prelude to her life in sketchy forms.

You can't go backward through time any more than you can gain ground by walking sideways. Little girls and little boys grow up, assuming characteristics of their own, leaving behind the toys and traits of their infancy. I would expect no less of our Teengirl, who is on the verge of leaving her teens behind like traces of a spent childhood.

*　　*　　*

Phases of an emerging personality create landscapes of their own, but when the difficult years of breaking the molds that confine us are past, we often remember with warmth those who helped us through them, as I remember big sisters who held my hand through hard weather and carried me past the mean years.

I suspect that Teengirl's sensibilities will one day find the same gentle ground of memory and return with an attitude of embracement, reaching across from her parallel world into ours and gracing us once more with her presence.

Dependence and independence are not always mutually exclusive in a society that dreams of individual freedom within an altruistic culture.

Teengirl is always welcome in our world, and I know she'll return to it if only for a visit.

Meanwhile, if you should see her, tell her Grandpa says hello.
EMTNSTR

## ACKNOWLEDGMENTS

Many, many thanks to my friends who have, over the years, shared their stories of raising their children. Their willingness to listen, to reveal their doubts, and to share their joys has proven to be invaluable and everything wonderful about friendship.

To my husband, Joel, for his wise and clear guidance. But most especially for his support as I pursue the many projects that seem to cross my path.

And to my daughter, Michelle, who amazes me with her bravery, her dedication to her beliefs, and her fierce independence.

—Joan

\*    \*    \*

To my husband Phil, for not letting this project die, always reminding me that these were incredible, important stories that would and should find an audience. His encouragement and support were paramount to my seeing this labor of love through to the end.

To Amy, my sister and my daughter's namesake, for providing support, resources, and research on what was going on with parents in her community. In addition, Amy was the conduit to one of our wonderful writers, Jeanne Aufmuth.

To the many members of the Renalds clan, spread far and wide, for their encouragement over the past 3 -plus years. A special mention to my dear friend Maureen Gomberg, whose faith and almost-constant prodding really made a difference. Now I know why you keep winning sales awards!

And lastly, to the two most inspiring women in my life: my mother Molly Renalds for teaching me the fine art of letting go (among many, many other things). I thank you. And to my daughter Amy, who has unselfishly chosen to follow the path of her grandmother by helping those less fortunate: I could not be prouder of you. —Julie

\* \* \*

Thanks to Julie and Joan for bringing me in on this worthwhile project. What a long journey it's been to get here. We are quite a team!

Special thanks to Elizabeth Fishel and the Wednesday Writers who supported my efforts on this book over the last couple of years. My deepest thanks to Martha Loeffler, a wonderful role model—both as a writer and as a human being. I'm so glad we met over a manuscript on a crowded plane.

To my husband, Bruce, who rode the waves of excitement and frustration along with me as this project took shape: thanks for being my biggest fan.

To all the "Mommies": Thank you for listening to me read my stories, and for all the "atta girls" over the years. You are treasures, every one.

Thank you to my sister, Susie Elkind, for her sharp eyes and her red pencil.

Caitlin, Christian, Myles, Laurel, James and Ashley: you guys are the best.

To little Madeleine Olivia, who has brought me boundless joy just by being here, thanks for giving me another chance to make a nest. —Risa

# PERMISSIONS

Ronnie Caplane, "The Good-bye Girl" appeared in the *Mont-clarion*, February, 2000.

John Leland, "Out in the World (and Barely a Word)" appeared in the *New York Times*, July 29, 2007. Reprinted with permission from the *New York Times*.

C.W. Nevius, "When a Son Heads off to College" appeared in the *San Francisco Chronicle*, August 19, 2005.

Risa Nye, "One by One" appeared in the *Head-Royce Magazine*, Winter, 2006.

Al Martinez, "A Bittersweet Parting, an Empty Nest" appeared in the *Los Angeles Times*, September 3, 2004.

Al Martinez, "Her Independent Streak Runs at the Speed of Life" appeared in the *Los Angeles Times*, October 24, 2005.

William Morrow and Company, Inc.: "Laura's Room," from *No Place Like Home* by Linda Weltner. Copyright © 1998 by Linda Weltner. Reprinted with permission from William Morrow and Company, Inc.

# CONTRIBUTORS

JEANNE AUFMUTH is the mother of two daughters, the step-mother of two stepdaughters, and the grandmother of a spirited granddaughter. She is the lead film critic for the *Palo Alto Weekly* and the acting President of the San Francisco Film Critics Circle. Her reviews can be found on www.paloaltoonline.com and www.aufmuth.com. Jeanne strives to keep mind and body active through extensive travel and a series of rousing contact sports, including ice hockey, sword fighting, and kickboxing. The gentler side is placated with stripping, yoga, and watercolor.

RONNIE CAPLANE lives in Piedmont, California, where she was a weekly columnist for several Knight-Ridder papers. Her essays have appeared in many publications, including the *Chicago Tribune*, *Cleveland Plain Dealer*, *San Francisco Chronicle*, *Detroit Free Press*, *Jewish Bulletin of Northern California* (now known as *J Weekly*), and several anthologies. By day she is an attorney.

JOAN TAYLOR CEHN has worked in the healthcare field for many years as a speech pathologist and administrator. After her daughter's departure for college, she became involved in the organization of Ms. Renalds' parent support group. After a brief retirement, she has returned to her career with renewed interest and perspective. Her daughter is currently a student at a private midwestern university. She and her husband live in Oakland, California.

WENDY COHEN is back where she belongs—in Oakland, California—working and raising a wonderful adopted son and getting ready for another empty nest.

BILL COY is a management consultant, a teacher at the University of San Francisco, and a licensed marriage and family therapist. In his professional life he has worked for both the Catholic Diocese of Oakland and Industrial Light & Magic, thereby being the only consultant known to have facilitated meetings at both the Vatican and Skywalker Ranch. He is the father of David and the stepfather of Jeremy, Daniel, and Liz. He and his wife, Nancy, live in Oakland, California.

ELIZABETH FISHEL is the author of four books, including *Sisters* and *Reunion*, and the co-editor (with Terri Hinte) of two anthologies, *Wednesday Writers* and *Something That Matters*. She has also written widely for magazines, such as *Vogue, Oprah's O, Redbook, Parents, Family Circle*, and she was a contributing editor at *Child*. She teaches writing at UC Berkeley Extension and the UC Berkeley Graduate School of Journalism and also holds private classes on Wednesday and Friday mornings. She lives in Oakland with her husband, and they have two sons.

JOHN LELAND is a reporter on the national desk of the *New York Times*. A graduate of Columbia College, he has been a senior editor at *Newsweek*, editor-in-chief of *Details* magazine, and an original columnist at *SPIN*, and he has written for *Newsday, Rolling Stone, Vogue*, the *Face*, the *Village Voice*, and numerous other publications. He is also the author of two books, *Hip: The History*, an alternative history of American culture, and *Why Kerouac*

*Matters: The Lessons of 'On the Road' (They're Not What You Think)."* He lives in New York City with his wife, Risa. His son Jordan, the subject of his essay, is at press time doing nicely at the University of Wisconsin at Madison. So far, so good.

JOANNE LEVY-PREWITT is an independent college advisor working with high school students in the San Francisco Bay Area. A former teacher, Joanne is also a short-fiction writer. She writes a weekly, nationally syndicated column called "College Bound," which can be read in newspapers across the United States. She has one son who is a college senior, and she lives with her husband in the Bay Area. Contact Joanne at: jklprewitt@gmail.com.

MARTHA LOEFFLER, a retired social worker (UC Berkeley, 1941) started her second career, as a writer, in 1985, when she was 65 years old. Her work has appeared in newspapers and magazines and has won many awards. She is the author of three books, including *Boats in the Night*, about the rescue of Jews during the Holocaust, which is widely used in schools around the country. She is working on her fourth book, and at the age of 87, she currently teaches a writing workshop for senior citizens who are working on their memoirs. She is a member of The National League of American Pen Women.

AL MARTINEZ is an award-winning columnist and feature writer with the *Los Angeles Times*. Among many other honors, he was named Journalist of the Year by the Society of Professional Journalists (1996), and won the Pulitzer Prize Gold Medal for Meritorious Public Services in 1994. A San Francisco Bay Area native and father of three, he is also the author of ten books, the creator of three network television series, and was an Emmy nominee for the TV movie *Out on the Edge*. He contributed to the *Los Angeles Times* metro teams that won Pulitzer Prizes following coverage of the L.A. riots in 1993 and the earthquake in 1994. His outstanding contributions to human relations through his work have been acknowledged by many organizations throughout his journalistic career.

PAM SIMONSEN MURAMATSU is a proud Seattle-area native. She earned her nursing degree, married her high school sweetheart, and helped him through dental school. She retired from nursing to be a full-time mom to her two sons. She currently resides in Des Moines, Washington, with her husband, John, and her dog, Butch.

C.W. NEVIUS is a Pulitzer Prize-nominated columnist who has written about sports, movies, and parenthood, among other topics, for the *San Francisco Chronicle*. He has two children, both of whom are just about to put their parents into the empty nest phase (hopefully). His book *Crouching Toddler, Hidden Father* is available at most bookstores.

RISA NYE writes essays and articles for Bay Area publications. She is also the author of *Road Scholar*, a journal for college-bound students. In addition, she is a contributor to the Chicken Soup for the Soul Series and the recently published anthology *Something that Matters: Life, Love, and Unexpected Adventures in the Middle of the Journey*. She has been a college counselor for many years. Her newest title is "Grannie," which delights her in new and unexpected ways. She and her husband live in Oakland, California.

MARILYN O'MALLEY was born in Honolulu, grew up on military bases, and has lived in the northwest for thirty years. She is a graduate of Portland State University, where she studied psychology and sociology. She's a vocalist and rhythm guitarist, as well as a singer-songwriter. She performed with a number of Irish bands in Oregon and Washington, and also enjoys gardening, hiking, and rafting wild rivers. Marilyn is currently writing a book about restoring cow pastures to the native plants of Klickitat County, Washington, and how several major transitions in mid-life brought her to a new beginning in the High Prairie.

JOAN PASSMAN has survived the raising and launching of both a daughter and a son, and now enjoys three grandchildren. It's much easier having children a generation removed. She was a first-grade teacher for many years and is currently involved in rewarding volunteer work. Joan and her family live in various cities in California.

LINDA LEE PETERSON is the cofounder of a marketing communications firm with offices in the San Francisco Bay Area and Philadelphia. Before her first mystery novel, *Edited to Death*, was published in 2005, she had written the text for a number of nonfiction books including two books for HarperCollins, *Linens* and *Candles*, and *On Flowers* for Chronicle Books. She is completing work on her second mystery, *The Devil's Interval*. Linda and her husband, a judge, live in Lafayette, California. She is a graduate of Stanford University.

JULIE RENALDS has a daughter who graduated from a private university in New York, and also has two stepsons, Ben and Jake.

By day Julie is in business development for a software company in the San Francisco Bay Area. She enjoys running in the Oakland hills, reading, and spending time with her seven siblings, various nieces and nephews, and her mother, who is her "inspiration for all things mothering." She has formed a large network of other parents throughout the country who are experiencing the huge transition of downsizing (in terms of family members under one roof) and tremendously enjoys helping them over the bumpy parts. She can be reached at jarenalds@yahoo.com.

SHARON ROCKEY is a freelance writer and ghostwriter living in Portland, Oregon. www.webspinstudios.com. Her advice to moms: "Next time you tearfully pray to understand where you went wrong, and an inner voice secretly whispers that your child came into this world with their own baggage, keep it to yourself!"

ROQUE GUTIERREZ is a retired postal worker who has been writing most of his life. He has written three books and numerous short stories for children. The short stories have been published in various children's magazines and the books are pending. He is currently working on his fourth book, a young adult novel as well as an adult mystery. He is hoping a publisher soon discovers what they are missing and publishes him.

LAURA SHUMAKER is the mother of three boys, and has been an advocate for her autistic son, Matthew, and other disabled children in her community for almost twenty years. A regular contributor to NPR Perspectives, she is also a member of the distinguished Wednesday Writers Group of Berkeley, California, whose books of essays fund Breast Cancer Research. Her work has been published in the *San Francisco Chronicle*, the *Autism Perspective*, the *Contra Costa Times*, and *Guideposts Magazine*, and she has just completed a memoir about life with an autistic son. Laura lives in Lafayette, California with her husband, Peter, and her teenage boys.

RANSOM STEPHENS is a writer, physicist, public speaker, and the author of over two hundred articles in science journals, the electronics industry, and magazines on subjects ranging from global warming to parenting teenagers. As a graduate student he discovered a new type of matter, as a professor he was on the team that discovered the top quark, and as an engineer he led a high-tech commando team, but his greatest accomplishment was raising his daughter. Look for Ransom and Heather's story in *Fade to Pink: From Goth to Graduation* set to be released in April 2009. Contact him at www.ransomsnotes.com.

EVE YOUNG VISCONTI, a freelance writer, lives in Foster City, California. She has written numerous articles that have appeared in career publications, co-authored several training manuals, written movie reviews for a weekly newspaper, and done public relations writing and grant writing for nonprofit organizations.

LINDA WELTNER wrote the column "Ever So Humble" in the *Boston Globe* for nineteen years. The author of two young adult novels and two collections of columns, she has recently written "The Challenge of Childhood Diabetes: Family Strategies for Raising a Healthy Child" with her daughter, Laura Plunkett. She lives with her husband, Jack, a child psychiatrist, in Marblehead, Massachusetts.

"The Challenge of Childhood Diabetes: Family Strategies for Raising a Healthy Child," a week-by-week, month-by-month guide to diet, exercise, and coping with psychological stress can be purchased at www.challengeofdiabetes.com.

KATE WHEATMAN has worked as a career counselor, the director of a social service agency, an employee relations specialist, and as a recruiter. Most recently, she said good-bye to a twelve-year career in corporate communications to become a freelance writer. She lives outside San Francisco with her husband, daughter Rebecca, and daughter Laura, when she is home from college.

PHILIP WEINGROW is the father of two sons and the stepfather of one stepdaughter. He has written frequently for The Hills Newspaper Group, a division of Knight-Ridder, writing consumer articles involving residential sales. He is a native New Yorker and a graduate of The New School for Social Research. He has taught in the New York City and City of Berkeley Public School Systems. He is currently managing a real estate firm in the Montclair area of Oakland, California.